THE
HONEST
MUMS'
CLUB

THE HONEST MUMS' CLUB

Parenting.
Depression.
Cake.

HANNAH OAKLAND

DARTON · LONGMAN + TODD

**For Wes,
Who never gave up.
Thank you.
xxxx**

First published in 2016 by
Darton, Longman and Todd Ltd
1 Spencer Court
140–142 Wandsworth High Street
London SW18 4JJ

ISBN 978-0-232-53222-7

Cover: Gem West is the artist behind OhHelloBeau.
Connect with her on:
Instagram: @ohhellobeau
Twitter: @ohhellobeau
Facebook: www.facebook.com/ohhellobeau
Etsy: www.ohhellobeau.etsy.com

A catalogue record for this book is available from the British Library.

Designed and typeset by Judy Linard

Printed and bound in Great Britain by Bell & Bain, Glasgow

Contents

SPRING 147

On starting

I 've never had a problem with starting.

Finishing? That's a different story. Reams of to-do lists, half-completed art projects, and the mountain of books by my bed are proof of that. Six weeks ago I altered one of Elvie's curtains and gloried in my new found mastery over the sewing machine. It hangs proudly in her bedroom now. Only slightly squint. Its partner sits and waits. Meanwhile the window is covered by a makeshift selection of blankets, black fabric and sheets, which struggle to keep her in bed past six a.m..

I will finish it. One day. Probably.

I love the thrill of 'new'. I always have. The chance to start over. To get something right. There is nothing as simultaneously inspiring and terrifying as a brand new notebook, full of crisp empty pages. If only I could find the right one I'd be able to write my bestselling novel, or the journal that would drag me out of depression. Or the memory books to prove to my children that they have always been loved. Even in my darkest, grumpiest hours.

Starting is intoxicating. So much potential. Finishing has always been for other people. The ones who bother about the details. The ones who are somehow able to resist the call of shiny-and-new.

But now. Now. Dealing with the constant, mind-numbing relentlessness of bringing up two small children, I find myself actively searching for things that I can finish. For something, anything, that can be crossed off my to-do list without going straight back on it the next morning. For a sense of accomplishment in amidst the endlessness. For the chance to finally reach the end of a sentence. Even a thought.

And so I find myself here. Starting something new. Again. And hoping that this time, I'll finish.

Because this time there's one big difference. This time I've been afraid to start.

I've been talking about writing a book for years now. Listening to other people tell me that I should. And not doing anything about it. Because I'm scared. But here we are. Finally. Words on paper. Emails to publishers. Working through my story. Putting myself out there. Dealing with the fear, and the shame, and the niggling certainty that I'll end up flat on my face.

Depression is a beast. Parenting is relentless. Between them they've drained out all my fun. All my energy. All my hope. All my brave.

And yet here I am. Starting. Being as brave as I can manage, and as hopeful as I dare.

Some days, that's all you can do.

SUMMER

June

Moonlight.

Imagine that you're watching YouTube videos. Kittens, probably. Being unbearably cute. Doing things that no animal has ever done before. Playing the violin. Tap dancing. Blowing out candles. You get the picture.

Initially, you're genuinely impressed. Perhaps you're even considering getting a kitten of your own. Gradually your interest wanes and your brain starts to wander. By the time you reach the thirty-fourth video, your mouth is smiling but your eyes have glazed over while your brain double-checks your shopping list and wonders if you remembered to series link *The Great British Bake Off*.

That is what has become of my life. Slowly but surely it's looking less like actually living and more like a numb, not-really-here-right-now-but-hopefully-still-making-the-appropriate-facial-expressions attempt at an existence. Depression's got that nailed. Except that it's not kittens. Or YouTube. It's my family. It's real. And it's shit.

Sometimes I can convince myself that I'm in control of my demons. That the therapy is just a formality. To keep the doctor happy. Today is not one of those days. This morning, during the how-many-people-can-we-fit-in-one-bed ritual that has come to signal the start of our day, I was numb. The children were adorable. Joel babbling. Elvie playing along. Big dribbly, slobbering baby kisses all over my face. I smiled. I may even have made some appropriate noises. But I felt nothing. Other than guilt. Which is fun.

There are occasions where I'm not so numb. Then, I'm mostly angry. Irrationally, furiously angry – at Wes, or the children, or myself. Or anyone else who gets in my way. It's exhausting. And fairly toxic. Bizarrely, I'm clinging to it as a good omen. At least I feel something. I don't remember that last time around. When I think back to Elvie's first months, my memories consist mostly of shrugging my shoulders and staring blankly at the walls. Having an opinion, of any kind, just took too much effort.

This time, when I saw the doctor, he took a full set of bloods to rule out any physical cause for my depression. The results came back today. Completely clear. Which means that there won't be a magic pill. I'm not horribly deficient in any crucial vitamins. I'm not anaemic after all. Neither do I have thyroid problems.

I know that I should be glad. But those blood tests were my get-out. My last chance to imagine that I'm not *really* depressed. To convince myself that I have a physical problem, with a simple medical solution. Now that chance is gone. I suspect my doctor has known all along, which is why he signed me up for therapy as well. 'Just in case.' Sneaky.

And so, I find myself going backwards. Back to the doctors. Back to therapy. Back to really, truly admitting that I'm in the same stinking, miserable place all over again. I hate backwards. It's not my style. I've fought this once, I've beat it once and it feels desperately unfair to be starting all over again. I'm not sure that I have the energy for the fight. Not right now.

I've had distractions today. Wonderful friends coming round for playdates and listening to me moan. Elvie's 'starting nursery' session this afternoon. Being around other people. Keeping busy. Anything to stop my brain spiralling into those pointless, hateful little circles.

But still the numbness. And the anger. The tears. Always

the tears. Waiting just below the surface. I'm trying to carry on. Doing the everyday things – tying tomato plants to sticks, washing up, making lunch, putting the baby down for his nap. Eventually I was too exhausted, and stared blankly into space while Wes made dinner.

There is so much to be thankful for. I know. I do. One look at my beautiful family, our little home or our friends can tell me that. But it's so hard to see it in the dark.

Last year, on a church camp in the woods, we ventured outside for the traditional late-night bonfire. At least, we were planning to – until Elvie was scared of the dark. Eventually I managed to persuade her that we were going 'for a walk with the moon', which appealed sufficiently to her imagination to convince her to try. And she loved it. Of course.

These essays. This book. These are my attempts at walking with the moon. One more attempt to look up for long enough to find the way ahead. To use my creativity to fight off the fear and the blackness. I'm told that the moon is most visible when everything is really, really dark.

On that basis, it shouldn't be too hard to find.

The truth/something beautiful.

Last night Wes and I went to a gig at Westonbirt Arboretum. Paloma Faith. Outside. In the rain. Don't be fooled into jealousy over my wildly glamorous life – it is quite literally years since we went to a gig. Or the cinema. Or pretty much anywhere. But yesterday we put on our wellies and our raincoats and our we-don't-mind-the-weather faces, and we went. As a Father's Day present for Wes and, let's be honest, a chance to get out of the house and leave the kids with their grandparents. For an entire evening. Hoorah.

I should point out that there's only one of Ms Faith's

songs that I know well enough to sing along to. I had been dutifully humming it all day as preparation. Midway through the afternoon I realised how perfectly it would fit into an essay about the current state of my brain. I was onto something. It would be effortless – with all the appearance of having a musical epiphany whilst freezing my toes off in a forest. I'm pretty sure it's the kind of writing that would win awards.

She didn't play the song. Seriously. Even Paloma Faith is trying to keep me honest. (It could be that her set list had nothing to do with me, and was based on the fact that she has a new album to test out. Whatever.)

Bear with me while I shoe-horn in the pertinent line from the song that was never played. It'll be seamless. (Really, I'm fine about the whole thing. Honest.) It goes a little something like this ...

Do you want the truth or something beautiful?

That lyric leaps out of the radio at me every time I hear it. Those have felt like my options for the longest time. Truth or beauty. Being honest or keeping everyone happy. Letting people see me as I truly am, or maintaining my carefully polished veneer of a woman-in-control. The truth, with all its messiness, brokenness and vulnerability has never felt like a viable option.

Motherhood changed all that for me. Not initially, admittedly – the temptation to project the image of the perfect, blissed-out mother was just too strong. I'm not sure it ever worked. Not really. But I was damned if anyone was going to know just how badly I was failing.

I dragged my heels through a year of post-natal depression and everyone thought I was fine. Nobody saw the times I sat and sobbed. The times I couldn't bring myself to cook, or tidy, or leave the house. I didn't tell anyone how desperately I needed to run. To start over again. Somewhere far, far away. Nobody knew that, as far as I was concerned, my baby would be better off raised by somebody else. Anybody else. That's an ugly, awkward kind of truth.

Now, with two children, as depression settles itself in for another innings, I have a problem. I want my babies to be sure of themselves. To be confident. And brave. To know that they are enough, just as they are. That no matter how painful or inconvenient their truths, they are worth listening to and worth loving. There's only one way that can happen.

You can't teach something that you don't understand. I can only help them if I can help myself. If I can be brave, even when I'm afraid. If I learn that I am enough, just as I am, if I share my truths, and accept them, and love myself anyway. Which is hard. Very hard. Probably not impossible, but very, very close.

So this is it. This is me. Studying honesty and openness and vulnerability, as best I can, in the hope of passing those gifts on to these two tiny humans that I've brought into this world. I'm reading books and subscribing to blogs and listening to wise, generous friends. I'm talking. I'm sharing. In real life and in writing. With my family and friends. Tiny little steps towards an understanding that my truth *is* something beautiful. There is no either/or.

Skirts are not pyjamas.

Elvie wore a skirt to bed tonight. Not a pyjama skirt, if such a thing exists, but a regular daytime skirt. Purple and frilly. Not for the first time, either. Over the last few nights we've found her, fast asleep, pyjama shorts abandoned on the floor, replaced by a skirt she's selected at random from her wardrobe. Occasionally she also discards her nappy pants. Bad news.

Even on the nights when her pyjamas stay put, there have been screams and tears at bedtime over her newfound, desperate desire to challenge the boundaries of nightwear. Toddlers are feisty, this one more than most.

Tonight was different. Tonight we chose her skirt together. As bedtime loomed, I tried to work out exactly why I was so deeply bothered by what my two-year-old chooses to sleep in. And honestly, it has nothing to do with the skirt. Or Elvie. It has everything to do with control. And me.

My depression has three main triggers: tiredness, stress and feeling out of control. Which is unfortunate. Given my current status as mother-of-two-small-children, those are basically my default emotional settings. The areas that I try to control are usually a practical outworking of my state of mind. On a positive day, I'll try to keep on top of the washing, our finances and the state of the kitchen. Normal things. Useful, even.

If I'm feeling low, then everything is fair game. And anyone can push me over the edge. A baby who skips a nap, a husband who didn't empty the bins, a toddler daring to play with more than one toy at once – or an inappropriate choice of nightwear.

It's a vicious circle. I feel the control slipping through my fingers, and so I invent and enforce hundreds of pointless rules. Loudly and repeatedly. Until I'm stressed out, shattered and broken. This circle needs smashing to pieces. Fast.

One of the things I love most about my Elvie is her uniqueness. She is, as some of our more diplomatic friends phrase it, a bit of a quirk. Uninhibited, exuberant and completely bonkers. Everything in me wants to nurture that quirk and encourage her to grow into herself, with all the dodgy foreign accents, unexpected clothing choices, and dancing on tables that will entail. I'm bracing myself for some interesting school reports.

But when I'm fighting the waves of depression, I try to control her and her oversized personality. She is so like me as a child and perhaps, subconsciously, I'm trying to stop her becoming like me as an adult. Trying to toughen her up and teach her that she can't always get what she wants. That she can't always do what she wants. My fear is that she'll end up learning that she can't be loved as she is.

Last week we were preparing for our first 'starting nursery' session. I was doing my best to take control of the situation. Wiping the crumbs from her face, trying to brush her hair into some kind of recognisable style. Not for her sake, but for mine. To show the nursery teacher what a responsible mother I am. How well I'm raising my child.

Midway through the pigtailing, she looked at me and said 'Mummy, stop it. I just want to go as I am.' Which stopped me in my tracks. Of course it's possible that she just wanted to avoid any further hair brushing. Whatever her reasoning, it worked.

Some things are worth controlling. Elvie is absolutely not one of them. I am determined to let her be herself. Even if that means dealing with some of my issues. And some slightly unorthodox pyjamas.

Why global warming is not (entirely) my fault. Promise.

I'm planning a christening for the children. (Or a baptism, or dedication. I'm not sure of the exact terminology just yet. I'm calling it a christening for now, because that's a word I understand. More importantly, so do my grandparents. And I'd really like them to come.)

We've left it later than most. Within a month of the

big day the children will turn three and one respectively. Apparently the usual practice is to do it a little earlier. As an especially dear friend said of Elvie at the weekend, 'I'm her godmother. Or at least I will be, if they ever get her christened.' Point taken.

My main problem is this. As a rule, christenings seem to involve parties. And I don't like throwing parties. For myself, or, in fact, at all. I love going to parties. It's just the hosting that I can't handle. The feeling that, unless everyone has 'the-best-time-ever' very loudly and very obviously, it's all an epic fail.

There are plenty of other scenarios that would constitute an epic fail: bad weather, a vomiting child, not having enough plates, running out of napkins, the icing clashing with the bunting, any lull in conversation, however brief. It's excruciating. And I bring it all upon myself. If I have invited these people, I must ensure that they are happy. Preferably ecstatic. For the entire duration of their visit.

I know that I am not responsible for absolutely everyone's happiness absolutely all of the time. Except that I don't. And so I apologise for absolutely everything. Because whatever happened, it was almost certainly my fault. Somehow.

Rain on your holiday? All my fault. Murray crashing out of Wimbledon? All my fault. Global warming? All my fault. No really, I leave the lights on. A lot.

Sometimes it all feels very worthy. Noble, even. I'm sure that sometimes it comes across as servant-heartedness or humility, or an eagerness to please. It can, on occasion, feel productive. Positive. After all, it's good to take responsibility for our actions – Brownies taught me that. (They also taught me to dance round toadstools and go peering into ponds for elves. On reflection, it wasn't all golden.) But there's a darker side to all this fretting and blame-taking and worthiness. And it's this. I don't do anything.

It makes sense. On some deeply misguided level. If I

can't do everything, then why bother doing anything? At all? Because whatever I do, it won't be good enough.

I can't take away your pain after a brutal breakup, so why would I invite you round for dinner? I can't prevent your miscarriage, so what good will a bunch of flowers do? I can't bring back your mum, so how would a letter help? And, crucially, if I can't guarantee the sunshine, why would I invite you into my garden for a christening party?

It's crippling. I suspect that I've missed out on more than just party-hosting over the years as a result.

At its very core, this whole approach to life is driven by fear and selfishness. Which is hard to admit when I've styled it out as worthy, caring and self-deprecating for as long as I can remember. If I take not-being-responsible-for-everything to its logical conclusion, the world does not, in fact, revolve around me. Which is unpleasant.

Not for long. Thankfully. After the initial bitterness of discovering that you are not the centre of the universe, it's liberating. At least, it has been for me. I am not responsible for all the pain of the world. Neither am I responsible for all its joy. So I should probably stop taking myself and my plans so seriously, and live a little.

I'm planning the christening. I'm inviting people round. In spite of everything. Our cutlery doesn't match, our floor won't be clean, and I certainly can't fix your problems. It might even rain. Never mind. Let's just hang out. I suspect that's all you wanted anyway.

Bedtime is a four letter word.

Wes is away this week. With work. For four days. Leaving four evenings, four nights and four bedtimes for me, my two tinies and a guinea pig who's holidaying in our garden.

I'm not Carol Vorderman. Not by a long shot. But even by my reckoning, 2 children + travelling rodent + bedtime x 4 = madness.

There is something about bedtime that sucks every last morsel of joy out of the day. All the deep and meaningful conversations we've had, all the great listening I've managed, all the bonus points I thought I'd earned by switching Wimbledon over to CBeebies for twenty minutes ... when the clock strikes six they all turn to dust. Like some twisted parenting Cinderella story. Every. Single. Night.

Bedtime is a test of patience and a battle of wills. Strong wills. Theirs and mine. Nobody should have to clean a toddler's teeth whilst being bitten on the leg by a baby. At least, not every night. Definitely not without a comrade downstairs to put the kettle on. Or pour the gin. Single parents, I salute you. Really. This is one hell of a gig.

Before my babies arrived, I cherished the idea of family bedtimes. Curling up for cuddles with my clean, sleepy children. Sharing stories and prayers, chatting about our days. Maybe a glass of milk. Some fairy lights. A rocking chair. Never did I imagine the epic toddler meltdown because Mummy only has the energy for one verse of 'Away in a Manger'. In June, for goodness sake. Or that the baby would shut his fingers in a drawer at exactly the same moment.

I certainly didn't foresee the moment when the sobbing toddler who won't stop hitting everyone gets sent to bed without a story, only to fall asleep by herself before Mummy has chance to sneak back in and hold her and tell her that she is loved. Which is exactly what happened tonight.

The fact of the matter is this; when Wes goes away, I panic. So do the children. And no matter how well we cope during daylight hours, bedtime turns us all into crazy people. I wish I could say that I rise above the chaos. That I don't join in the shouting and the screaming and the irrational behaviour. But I do. Most nights. And I'm surprised when that doesn't solve the problem. They'll let anyone have kids these days.

I don't like it. They don't either. But I have no idea what else to do. There doesn't seem to be a quick fix. Certainly not one that I've found. I'm just counting to ten, taking deep breaths and trying again. It hasn't worked so far. Still, there's always tomorrow. Or the next day. Or the next. Three nights to go. Until then, I'm just praying they sleep well.

And pouring my own gin.

Tea and cake and guinea pigs.

Elvie was barely twenty four hours old when we came home from hospital. Exhausted. Besotted. More than a little overwhelmed. And, in amongst all the white-blanketed, pain-killered, half-asleep serenity, I was terrified.

In the last few weeks of pregnancy I'd folded and refolded her tiny clothes. I'd googled the signs of early labour, and drunk pints of raspberry leaf tea. I'd spent hours trawling through obscure parenting forums that I would never visit again. What I hadn't done was give much thought to what would happen after the birth. When she was actually here.

After a couple of weeks the initial tide of visitors slowed, Mum went home, and I stopped posting new pictures on Facebook every hour. Wes's paternity leave came to an end, and suddenly it was just me and the baby. All day. For days on end.

I expected a lot from this new phase of my life. And I got it all. The first smiles and gurgles. Her little laughs. Her claps. Her waves. The insatiable curiosity and, eventually, those heartbreakingly precious first words. The wobbly little first steps, breadstick in hand. We spent hours curled up together. Feeding and napping in a little golden glow. Knowing without any doubt that I was utterly depended on and she was completely loved. These are the major selling points of new motherhood. And they're well worth selling. In those moments, everything feels like bliss.

That said, there was plenty that took me by surprise. No warning. No advance notice. The hours upon days of mind-numbing boredom that come with caring for a new baby. The endless repetition. Feed, burp, change, repeat. Over and over again. The havoc that sleep deprivation unleashes on your mind. The resentment that builds up as you watch your husband leave for work each morning, knowing that you won't get a hot cup of tea or an unaccompanied toilet break until he returns.

The combination of resentment, exhaustion and loneliness can be overpowering. It knocked me flat. Before I noticed it depression had snuck in, set up camp and eventually sent me crawling to the doctors to admit that I was in desperate need of some help.

I spent most of Elvie's first year in a dark cloud of numbness. I've shouted my way through most of Joel's. It doesn't feel good. I've been taking photographs obsessively, and poring over them. Again and again. Asking Wes whether I look 'happy enough.' Whether my babies will know how much they were loved.

There are positive moments every day, if I look hard enough. Even I know that. Some days there's not enough energy to look. That's ok. Those are the days to embrace the television and raid the chip shop. They usually turn out to be the highlight of the children's week. But even on the other days, there is always something to cling to.

Today was a disaster. Grumpy, up-too-early baby, grumpy, up-too-early Mummy and full-of-beans toddler is not a good combination. The synchronised falling-over-and-screaming routine at bath time was less than ideal. As was the baby-brother-in-a-headlock scenario this afternoon. I'm trying not to dwell on those things.

Instead, as I curl up in bed and pray with all my heart that Joel will sleep past 5 a.m., I am trying to focus on the joy. Wherever it was hiding. The wonder in Elvie's eyes as she played with the borrowed guinea pig. The grin on Joel's face when he saw his sister this morning. Watching him climb the staircase, all in one go, for the very first time. Elvie singing. Joel clapping along. Tea and cake on the sofa. The knowledge that, whatever the photos say, I'm doing the best that I possibly can right now.

I'm beginning to suspect that parenting will always be terrifying. That I will always be dealing with unknowns. Making it up as I go along. Trying to listen more than I shout. There are no words for how tough it is. At the moment I'm hanging on by my fingernails. But I have to believe that I can do it. That one day the black cloud will lift. That I'll look back over our photographs, guilt-free, and remember all the good bits. Tea and cake and guinea pigs. I can't wait.

July

How to talk to a Mummy.

This morning two women asked me if I am 'expecting'. I'm not. Awkward.

My response was calm, collected and mostly factual. A gentle monologue about babies who weigh more than 10lbs, split stomach muscles that will never heal, and the resulting stress on my lower back. With a fleeting nod to the exercises that the doctor has recommended, which I know I should have started already. Thanks for the encouragement.

The response inside my head was a little more emotional. A bucketful of asterisks, several less-than-generous comments on the physical state of the women themselves, and a whole heap of sobbing. Interestingly, neither response so much as hinted at the sheer volume of cake, ice cream and sweets that I've consumed over the last six months, in an ultimately ill-fated attempt to drive out my depression using nothing but the healing power of sugar.

The irony is that when I *am* pregnant, there's no room for doubt. You won't see me for four months whilst I hide on the sofa. Green-faced, miserable and craving anything made of ice. Once the sickness is over, the bump arrives. And I'm in danger of knocking over everyone within a 5 metre radius simply by turning around.

In the weeks before Joel was born, I was enormous. All bump. Looking to all intents and purposes as though someone had wedged a few footballs under my maternity top. Which, no matter how elasticated it was, couldn't cover my ludicrous stomach. I was stopped in the street by strangers, several times, so that they could tell me to my face how ridiculous my bump was. One old lady even beckoned me over to meet her friend with the words, 'That's the one I was telling you about. Have you ever seen anything like it?' Ouch.

Given the size of my forty-weeks-pregnant stomach, it's amazing that I don't still look ready to drop 10 months later. Especially after all that cake. And yet, this morning, the question hurt. So much so that I came home from toddler group via Matalan, with a shiny new belt. In the hopes of holding in my quite-clearly-hideous stomach. It didn't work.

Motherhood changes your body. Forever. Everyone knows that. It's an unavoidable truth. Unless you're a fan of those books that accuse you of letting down the sisterhood if you've not regained your inch-for-inch pre-baby dress size within three months. I had one of those. I even read it. Part of it, anyway. Needless to say, it's been recycled. Hopefully into toilet roll.

On the opposite side of the coin are women who wear their changed appearance with pride – as a constant reminder of the incredible feats that their body has accomplished. Stretch marks and bikinis? Why not. I like that idea. I like those women. A lot. I'd like to join their gang. But I'd also like a flatter stomach. And a one-piece swimsuit made of industrial strength lycra. Besides, I have two constant reminders of the incredible feats that my body has accomplished. Constant being the operative word.

I'll admit, it seems shallow. Why bother about my looks when I'm busy raising the next generation of world leaders, artists and entrepreneurs? Why worry about wobbly tummies, saggy boobs and chipped nail polish when I'm devoting my life to such a worthwhile, productive task? The honest answer is this: as a stay-at-home-mum, there are days when my appearance feels like the only scrap of identity that I have left.

I'm not earning a living anymore, my conversation revolves almost entirely around my children and, everywhere we go, I am introduced as 'Elvie and Joel's mum'. Most days the biggest statement I can make is which brand of nappies I carry in my changing bag. The way I look feels like a chance to reclaim who I was before. To remember that I'm still a person in my own right. To assert my individuality in the endless round of rhymetimes and messy play.

So when my favourite dress won't do up, or my skin is battered and blotchy from lack of sleep, or people tell me that I still look pregnant, it stings. It makes me feel smaller. Not physically, but in my soul. Smaller. Less worthy. Less like myself and more like the fat, frumpy, boring middle-aged woman that I secretly fear I'm becoming.

This is not a thinly-veiled plea for compliments. It's not all bad. My arms have certainly never been so toned – heavy babies have their advantages after all. It's more of a realisation. That right now, comments about my looks hit hard. And that probably, the underlying issue isn't my appearance at all, but my identity. In reality, I need somewhere else to find my self-worth. That's tough. And it takes an awful lot of energy. Which is in short supply when you're a parent of young children.

We're all in this together, as they say. And so, I beg of you, be gentle with your mummy friends. We know that our buttons don't meet in the middle, that our wrinkles are showing and that our clothes are a few seasons old. Whatever flaw you have spotted will be far more apparent to us. Don't comment on those things, however gently. Go deeper. I dare you.

Ask us how we're really doing. Us. Not the kids. What's inspiring us at the moment? What plans are we making for those mystical, far-off days when all the children are at school? Ask us about our dreams and our fears and our hopes. Not just about our babies. Perhaps then we'll start to believe that there is worth inside of us. In our minds. In our hearts. And our ideas. Not just in our bodies and the million ways that they've been ravaged by their incredible achievements.

For future reference, I'm not 'expecting'. Neither am I planning to be. If you could pass that on to everyone you meet, I'll be eternally grateful.

Feral isn't always bad. Right?

My children are borderline feral. At least, Elvie is. Joel can't even walk yet. Give him time.

Yesterday was impressive, even by her standards. In the morning I found her hiding at the back of the garden, munching the carrot she'd been sent to give to the guinea pig. Dirt, peel and all. Later, having left the room for approximately twenty-seven seconds, I returned to find her sitting astride her baby brother. Trying to 'ride him like a horse'. In the afternoon she decorated her face, her arms and most of her nice clean dress. With chocolate ice-cream.

So far, so good. But in the evening she really outshone herself. After church, and a communal shepherd's-pie dinner. During which she'd mostly refused to eat any peas, before running wild with her friends. Eventually I caught up with her, to suggest that perhaps she should use the toilet before the walk home. She gave me that look. The one that means trouble.

'Mummy, I just had a wee. On the floor.' Ah.

Having located, dried and cleaned the offending puddle I moved on to phase two of Operation Recover-The-Situation. Perhaps, I ventured, she could take her knickers off, so that I could give her some dry ones. Again, that look.

'Mummy, I already took my knickers off.' Ah.

If yours was the black mountain bike leaning against the pillar, I can only apologise. Apparently it bears a very close resemblance to a clothes horse.

This morning was business as usual at the toddler group summer picnic. Tearing around in nothing but her knickers, having soaked her entire outfit in a frenzy of water, bubbles and soap. Completely unfazed, she charged up and down the hill, flung herself and a plastic dolphin down the slide, and pushed her friends around on the ride-along cars. All accompanied by a wild, dirty cackle. Her 'beside-myself-with-glee' laugh. I may have used the phrase 'raised by wolves'. More than once.

In all honesty, it is these abandoned, wholehearted, borderline-feral moments that make my heart burst with pride. Watching her. Lost in the moment. Envying the freedom that she has to be so utterly herself. That glorious age when having fun is infinitely more important than what anyone else thinks. I look at her with tears stinging the backs of my eyes – wondering how long she can stay like this. How long it will take for the world, and growing up, to get in her way.

Wondering when the world, and growing up, got in my way.

Why do I worry so much about what other people think of me? How did that take so much control over my life? Why do I bury the parts of me that I fear people won't like, before anyone even has the chance to decide? When did keeping my clothes clean become more important than jumping in feet-first? When did taking a Facebook-profile-worthy-picture become more important than actually, really smiling?

I've lost it. Somewhere along the line. That joy that I see in my daughter. That carefree, this-is-who-I-am attitude that makes her eyes sparkle – with delight or rage in equal measure. She may only be two years old but she knows what makes her happy. And she runs with it. Literally.

I know that July is not the traditional time for resolutions. Never mind; here's one. I'm resolving to be a little more feral and a lot more free. To know, and try my very hardest to accept who I am and what makes me happy. To write more. Create more. Pointless, beautiful things. To dance in my kitchen. Paint my nails occasionally. Read more books. Drink more tea. Grow things. And eat them.

This time, I'm learning from my daughter. Because, whoever those wolves are, they're doing something right.

Fear-less.

Joel is fearless. Nothing seems to scare him at all. Not yet, anyway. He'll climb over anything, wander into the road, grab hold of strange animals. It may not be ideal, but there's no denying it's gutsy.

Today he met my sister and her husband. Over from Tanzania on a visit, they turned up at our house fresh off the plane. We've not seen Grace for nearly two years, and have never met Jastin, thanks to the vastly overenthusiastic Foreign Office visa policy. When they arrived this morning, Elvie was sceptical. Understandably. She took a while to warm up to Aunty Grace, who she hadn't seen since she was a baby, and was just about won over by Uncle Jastin by the time they had to leave.

Joel, on the other hand, was smitten from the moment he saw them. Despite never having set eyes on either of them before. Smiles. Cuddles. Using them as climbing frames, which is the highest accolade he can give. He was utterly fearless. I'd assumed that Elvie would be the same, and it was fascinating to see her hold back. Part of me is relieved – a healthy dose of potential-danger-awareness can only be a good thing. That's what stops children running out into oncoming traffic, or disappearing off by themselves. I hope.

The emphasis is on a *healthy* dose. One of the surest signs of my depression taking root is my irrational fears spiralling out of control. For months after Elvie was born, I was reluctant to let anyone else hold her. Anyone. Even Wes. Terrified of some vague, nonspecific tragedy. Certain that I'd spend the rest of my life hating myself for having let her go. Wes took her to B&Q one afternoon and rather than resting, I spent the entire time in a blind panic that I'd never see my baby again. The next day he went to Tesco. Elvie stayed with me – I just couldn't stand the fear.

My therapist had some great, common sense strategies for dealing with irrational anxiety. I still use them, and as a result this time round my depression has a much less anxious edge. I wish I could say the same about my overthinking. I worry so much about every upcoming event, however small, that I plan myself into a frenzy, trying to control absolutely every single element and then wind up cancelling or being so exhausted from worry that I don't enjoy it at all. No matter how great it is. That's something to work on. Or so the therapist says.

The children form the basis of most of my worries – my nightmares are forever portraying them as victims of tragic accidents, or screwed up forever by my awful depressive parenting. I worry that they won't find good friends, and they won't eat enough vegetables. That they'll never be happy. The list goes on. Ironically it is also the children who are pushing me to be less fearful. Their joy is inspiring. Their carefree attitude and their general air of madness. I don't want to miss out on life because I'm afraid. I'm fed up of all this nonsense. Goodness knows Wes is.

After I finished my treatment, the therapist asked me why one section of the questionnaire always scored a 10, regardless of the week's events. The *'I would always avoid certain situations due to a fear of a particular object or event'* question. He asked. And so I told him. I am completely, and utterly terrified of snakes. Not just won't-walk-through-the-reptile-house terrified, but literally unable to even look at one. No matter what kind. On the telly, in a book. Not even a toy snake. As one poor, unsuspecting university housemate discovered when she put a tiny rubber python on my shoulder one evening as a joke. Needless to say, it did not end well.

I couldn't tell him why I was so petrified of snakes, because I didn't know. (Although a recent re-viewing suggests that a childhood spent watching *Labyrinth* probably didn't help.) All I knew was that I avoided them like the plague. That they were evil. That they could kill me. And almost certainly would, given half a chance. In return for my honesty, he told me that my continued avoidance was making them seem like a much greater threat than they actually are. In short, if I wanted to overcome my fears, I needed to hang out with more snakes. Brilliant.

The problem is, I really did want to overcome my fears. I didn't want to hand them down to Elvie or Joel. I didn't want to be the lame mum who never showed them the reptile house, or didn't let them watch *The Jungle Book*. (Yep. Even cartoon snakes. Told you it was bad.) And so, very gradually, I tried. I stopped closing my eyes every time I saw an advert for *I'm a Celebrity ....* I stopped skipping all the snake-related pages in Elvie's library books. I took her to the Children's Centre, knowing full well that the Animal Magic people were coming. And I stayed in the room when they got the real, live, slithering snakes out. I watched the whole thing. From a distance. With a dangerously elevated heart rate and very sweaty palms.

Eventually, months later, I actually touched a snake. On holiday last year. I didn't hold it, or kiss it, or wrap it round my neck, but I touched it. I had shaky hands and massively irregular breathing, but I touched it. If I had to rank the proudest moments of my life, this would definitely make the top 10. Mostly because Elvie was watching and this year, when we went back, she touched that same snake. Touched it, stroked it, and talked to it. Completely unafraid. That's my girl.

The whole snake incident got me thinking. After I'd calmed down a bit, obviously. There are shed-loads of situations that I avoid, simply because I'm scared of them. What would happen if I stopped skirting around them, and just went for it? I'll never be fearless, but perhaps I could just listen to my fear-less?

And so I set myself a challenge: to do one thing each month that I'm afraid of. On the list so far – use my sewing machine, go camping and make pastry. I know. I bet your fears seem positively normal now. I'm also going to write. And share my writing. That's the big one. For me, anyway. Because, it seems, the things that scare me most are the things that I most want to do. The parts of myself that I most desperately want to let out. The parts that I'm most afraid of people judging. Failing is scarier than a snake. But, for the most part, people are kinder than we think.

If I can do it, anyone can. Most days I'm afraid to look behind the shower curtain in case someone's hiding in there. Seriously. I'll never be as fearless as my boy, but that's okay, I'm choosing, every day, to fear-less. One little tip-toe step at a time. Snakes, sewing machines and shower curtains. Here goes.

Pretty things and superglue.

Elvie broke something this morning. Something of mine. Nothing big or expensive. A white ceramic notepaper holder that's shaped like a birdhouse. Whimsical, completely pointless and very pretty. I like that sort of thing. I'd left the room for three minutes. Having the audacity to visit the bathroom unaccompanied. She wasn't even alone. Wes and

Joel were there. But she got herself wildly over-excited, as so often happens, and kicked the books on my bedside table. Which crashed into the birdhouse-notepaper-holder. Which hit the floor. It's now in pieces. Apparently our bedroom carpet is not as soft as it first appears.

I can glue it back together. I already checked – holding the broken fragments up against each other. There's only the tiniest piece missing. But that's not the point. It's not just a notepaper holder. These things never are. It was a present from my parents. A symbol of the calm, beautiful, uncluttered space that I'll live in one day – and the comfort that someone else believes in it too. It's a white-ceramic sign of more peaceful days ahead. Which explains why I was much sadder than was strictly necessary when I found it in pieces by the bed.

When I was pregnant with Elvie, I thought I was prepared for the Great Child Takeover. Ignorance is bliss. I knew I'd spend the rest of my days taking care of them and tending to their every need. I knew there would be tough times. I knew I'd be exhausted. I didn't realise that nothing would ever truly be mine – mine and nobody else's – ever again.

I didn't realise that a clean top lasts a maximum of twenty minutes before it's covered in snot, suncream and dribble. That there's no point washing my hair, because as soon as I step out of the shower I'll be grabbed by a baby who just took a bath in his breakfast. That I can't eat a meal without someone leaning on me, 'testing' my drink or trying to steal my food. That they pinch my bracelets and my makeup and my shoes. I certainly never imagined quite how much it is possible to achieve with only one free arm.

I'm permanently on call. Even during the sacred, tea-drinking evening hours when they're tucked up in bed. Whatever I'm doing is ready to be dropped at a moment's notice, to calm a teething baby or a toddler who's having a bad dream. Not even my body is my own anymore. The pregnancies and the births and the hormones and the breastfeeding and the split stomach muscles and, let's be honest, the cake, have taken an irreparable toll on whatever figure I once had.

On top of all that, it seems that my personal space is fair game as well. I've been reduced to a human climbing frame. Or leaning post, or cradle, or whatever they need at the time. I get way more than my recommended daily dose of hair pulling, poked eyes and bruises from their tiny knees and elbows. No wonder that so many of Wes's attempts at romance are met with an emphatic 'don't touch me.' Sometimes Mummy just needs some space.

As I learnt this morning, not even my little treasures are really mine. They're just toys. Waiting to be discovered and broken into pieces by my very own, home-grown pair of destroyers.

We moved into this house six months ago and I was determined that, as soon as Joel started sleeping in his nursery, our room would be a sanctuary. Free of children and their endless plastic tat. My own little den – a sparkly cave where I could sit and count my treasures. In peace. It hasn't worked. Joel sleeps in our bed most nights, and Elvie comes in like clockwork each morning, usually bearing gifts. Today there is a wind-up caterpillar, a purple hairslide and a painted wooden trinket box on my dressing table. None of which are mine.

As a Mummy, it's becoming impossible to carve out any space for myself. Or time for myself. Anything for myself, in fact. Relentless is the word that most new mums use. Often accompanied by wide, borderline terrified eyes as they realise exactly what they've let themselves in for. I'm assured that it does get better. Or different, at least. Just last night, Elvie pulled me close at bedtime to say, 'I love you Mama, we'll be friends forever.' And I melted. They certainly have their moments.

One day they'll both be at school, and I'll have hours to fill. One day they won't climb into my bed in the morning, and they'll have no interest in my treasures. They won't wear their breakfast, or use me as a stepladder. I hope. Maybe I'll miss it. Right now, I'm not convinced. But it's only for a season. They won't be small forever. I have to remember that. Somehow.

One day I'll have all the time in the world. Right now, if you need me, I'll be in my room with a notepaper holder and some superglue. At least until the baby cries.

Sabbath – and other things I'm bad at.

On Saturday, Elvie looked me straight in the eyes and said, 'You know, Mummy, everyone knows you're struggling to get through.' Seriously. She's not even three years old. I'd apply to Mensa on her behalf, but this afternoon she wanted to know why I won't let her swordfight with a goat. Swings and roundabouts.

Animal cruelty aside, it says something when my two-year-old has a better handle on my mental health than I do.

Wes came back on Friday from a week in Birmingham. A whole week. Seven long days, which is an awful lot of time to spend in sole charge of two small children. Even without dragging around a great black sack of depression. Throw that in as well, and a week can feel like an eternity.

Amazingly, we'd managed pretty well. We even had some fun. We made cupcakes, went to teddy bears' picnics, spent days in the garden with our friends and even, thanks to my wonderful, car-owning sister-in-law, visited the local science centre. So that Elvie could fulfil her heartfelt dream of being an 'experimenter.' Brilliant.

She had an incredible time. We all did.

When Wes finally returned, I relaxed. At last. To the point that I was entirely useless for at least 24 hours. Can't-remember-why-you-went-into-the-room, can't-remember-your-own-date-of-birth, can't-find-the-light-switch kind of useless. Everything was mush.

By Sunday, I felt a bit better. I decided that, as I'd survived by myself for an entire week, I've probably beaten the depression. I'm practically cured. So I can do all the things. Straight away. Of course.

We went into town. We went to church. I tackled a small mountain of christening planning. We stayed up late. I called friends. I invited an entire toddler group round to play this morning, and took both children shopping this afternoon. And now it's hit me. For the last few hours I've wondered why I'm getting so snappy and irritable. Why I'm in such a blind panic about Joel's slightly raised temperature. Why I'm so annoyed that the thunderstorms have knocked out our television signal. Why getting the children to bed at precisely 7 p.m. feels so important.

I'm exhausted. Turns out that two lie-ins don't cancel out an entire week by myself. When I'm exhausted, life is hard. For everyone, as my family will testify only too readily.

I never learn. One week of feeling better and I throw myself head-first at any opportunity that comes my way. And then I'm surprised when I burn out. Every. Single. Time. Everything I did this weekend was fun. All of it was worth doing. All of it is helping my recovery. But all of it at once is too much. By a long way.

At church yesterday, a friend preached on Sabbath. What that looks like. The idea of having one day in a week that feels totally different to the others. The revelation that actually, Sabbath isn't just another way to show our holiness; full of laws and rules and regulations. The ground-breaking suggestion that perhaps it's a concept that exists out of God's kindness. Because we need a rest. And He knows that. We physically can't keep on keeping on. Not all the time. You'd think I would take the hint.

One day my Sabbath will be about caring for other people. Inviting them into my home and feeding them. Visiting them in hospital. Baking them spectacular, four-tier cakes with home-made fondant decorations depicting their favourite pastimes. But not now.

For now, my Sabbath needs to be about taking care of myself. Listening when Wes offers to take the children off my hands. Sitting down with a cup of tea, rather than unloading the dishwasher. Using my evening to write, or water plants, or watch cooking programmes on the television. Because there is no way on earth that I can look after everyone else when I'm in pieces.

I might need to tattoo it on my forehead, but hopefully I'll get there in the end. I'll be lying low tomorrow. Looking after my poorly baby, my goat-fighting genius, and myself. Let's hope the telly's fixed.

Anger. Duplo. Role play. Or, a selection of activities that I have not enjoyed today.

I should preface this piece by saying that I love my babies fiercely. They are precious, beautiful and entirely amazing.

Bearing that in mind, I have a confession to make. Today, I couldn't stand the sight of them.

They weren't badly behaved. They weren't horribly clingy. They weren't even all that loud. Which is a miracle in itself. Truth is, they didn't need to *do* anything. Just being around them sent my blood pressure shooting off the scale. I would blame the depression, but I'm not convinced that's the only problem. I suspect that somewhere, buried in the darkness, every parent feels like this occasionally. We're just not supposed to admit it. Not in public, anyway.

I've been conducting some practical research. And it turns out that denying your feelings doesn't make them go away. Who knew? I was feeling all the things today. As long as those things started with 'No'. No, I don't want to play Duplo with you, if you're going to keep all the bricks to yourself and steal anything I manage to build. No, I don't want to spend an hour cooking you a nutritious meal if you're going to scream 'Take that silly stuff off my plate!' as soon as you set eyes on it. No, I don't want to rock you endlessly, in order to persuade you to take the nap that I would give my right arm for.

No. No. No. Just no.

Today, the main culprit was Elvie. My wonderful, bonkers girl. Who picked flowers and a baby pear from other people's gardens as a gift for the friends that we visited yesterday. And took off every scrap of her clothes within minutes of arriving to fling herself into their paddling pool. Who spent an hour this morning building a 'clambo slombo' out of Duplo. (Your guess is as good as mine.) Who asked me to tell her a story about 'Salimo the boy who ate a banana' and distracted herself by pretending to be Peter Rabbit before I'd even thought up an opening line.

She's incredible. A one-off. A real force of nature. She's also very hard work. Nobody can wind me up the way that Elvie does – mostly because she's a miniature version of myself. Also because she's two years old, and that's tough all round. And, to be honest, because I'd rather be reading a good book with a slice of cake than answering her relentless questions and starring in her constantly-evolving role plays. I'm exhausted. More than exhausted, most of the time.

And when Mummy gets exhausted, Mummy gets angry. Really angry. Often completely out of the blue, because someone has finally pushed her that little bit too far. There's not a lot of distance between 'trying-to-stay-calm' and 'crazy-angry-mummy'. Or a lot of warning. Shouting, however? There's plenty of that.

Most of the time I don't feel as though I can control it. Like it's not a choice I'm consciously making. Physically or emotionally. But I can usually keep a lid on it in public. Funny how that happens.

This afternoon, Elvie had an epic toilet-related accident. The worst possible kind. Whilst we were at church. Whilst she was playing with her friends. Having so much fun that she didn't notice what was happening. And then hiding out of sheer embarrassment. When I eventually found her, crouching behind a stairgate, I was furious.

Furious that she hadn't got to me in time. Furious that she was making my already-horrid day even harder. Furious that Wes was at work, surrounded by actual grown-ups, and not around to help. Friends arrived with spare underwear almost instantly, but there was still the clean-up to tackle.

I was so angry that I almost dragged her into the toilets. And proceeded to tell her in no uncertain terms how ridiculous her behaviour was, how upset she'd made me, and how she was a big girl now who should know better. She didn't say much. A few minutes in to my rant, I heard voices chatting outside the toilets, remembered that sound waves travel both ways, and set about getting a grip.

Five minutes later Elvie was dancing, singing and jumping up and down with her friends. I felt like I'd been punched in the stomach. With a great big shiny silver knuckleduster of shame. I knew that I'd overreacted. And that I'd only managed to calm down because I was afraid of what my friends would think of me. When had that become more important than my little girl?

This has been brewing for a while. So to speak. I lose my

temper far too often. I see the confusion written all over her face when I shout. I know that it only makes her behaviour worse. I've blamed it on my depression. There's an element of truth in that – I have much less patience and a lot less energy to deal with everyday problems. But it's not good enough. Not anymore.

I am a good parent. I think. I try my absolute best. But some days it's all too much. I marvel every time someone says that they can't imagine life without their children. Really? Either they're lying, or they have some serious undiagnosed amnesia. I find it all too easy to recall a life when I could go to the toilet by myself, or eat a meal without wearing it. A life where I could get up in my own time. And stay in my bed all night. Perhaps that's just me.

This evening, during dinner, we embarked upon another of our seemingly endless role plays. She was Mummy, I was Elvie, and we re-enacted in frighteningly elaborate detail the moment when we bought candyfloss from the vending machine on holiday. She remembered everything. Word for word. A throwaway conversation from two weeks ago.

Initially I was delighted – she obviously cherished the memories of our time away as much as I did. Those candyfloss covered moments had been precious. As I smiled, she moved on to another scenario. She was still playing Mummy, but this time she was telling Joel off and, as she gathered momentum, I heard all the phrases that I hate myself for using. Just falling out of her mouth. As though that's a perfectly normal way to talk to people. I've convinced myself that because she's so young, she won't remember any of this. Guess what. She does.

When she's frustrated, she shouts. And screams. Like any two-year-old. Except that all the words are mine. Every time she shouts, I hear myself. And every time I tell her off for shouting I feel like a hypocrite. Every time she apologises with those big confused eyes, I vow that I'll never raise my voice again. But I do. Over and over and over.

I'm done with it. I can't bear the guilt and the shame and the fear that I'm trampling all over her beautiful little personality.

I apologised to Elvie this afternoon. I told her that I was wrong, and that I love her. She smiled and told me that she loves me too. She's given me another chance. My biggest fear is that one day, those chances will run out. It doesn't bear thinking about.

Never in a million years would I wish my children away. Not for good, anyway. It's just that sometimes I really, really need a break. And pretending otherwise is doing me no favours.

One day I'll show this book to my babies. When they're old enough to understand, and I'm right next to them to explain. Because one day they might be parents too, and I can't bear the thought of them feeling crushed by impossible expectations of perfection. I'd rather tell them the truth. Warts and all. I'd rather they knew that sometimes I just want to curl up by myself and finish a train of thought. To cook something that isn't spaghetti bolognese or tuna pasta. To have an uninterrupted conversation with my husband. Because I'd put money on the fact that one day, they'll feel the same. I want them to know that, as far as I'm concerned, that's completely normal. And absolutely ok.

The anger? Not so much. Not okay. Not anymore.

Hold me to it. Please.

August

Why I'm not sold on the quick-fix. But I do love Cinderella.

I watched CBeebies with the children this evening. We love a bit of CBeebies. Well, they do. I mostly relish the opportunity that it provides for a sit-down. Occasionally even the chance to make dinner. By myself. I basically owe my sanity to whoever created this little oasis of parental calm. They deserve a Nobel Peace Prize. Or a Snickers, at least.

Brilliant as they most definitely are, it's possible that the big bosses at CBeebies Towers could benefit from a few basic lessons in scheduling. Today they showed their panto. In August. Nothing like a rousing, 'Merry Christmas everyone!' while you're finishing your ice lolly.

Elvie was delighted. Her heroine Nina, of *Nina and the Neurons* toddler-science-telly fame, was playing Cinderella. That sold it for her. She was all in. Christmas in summer? No problem. She sat spellbound, watching the entire show in a daze of misty-eyed amazement. Needless to say, I had to be Prince Charming at story time tonight.

I've always loved fairy stories, but this one has a very special place in my heart. It always has done, ever since I was born. Mum went into labour with me four weeks prematurely, in the theatre, watching a performance of *Cinderella*. That's what her friends who came to meet me in the hospital called me when I was born. Cinderella. I'm no psychologist, but I'm blaming my love of sky-high, beautiful, thoroughly impractical shoes on the circumstances of my birth.

All things considered, I didn't mind sitting through the pantomime this afternoon. Even in August. I'm always up for a fairy tale. There's just one thing that bothers me. And my inner feminist. And my hopes for my daughter.

Here it is. Cinderella's in a fix. They've stolen her invitation and ripped up her dress. She doesn't have any appropriate footwear. She'll never get to meet the prince, which is obviously tragic, because her life would be worthless without him. My dilemma is this - every time the story is told, all she has to do is cry. Mutter something about how badly she wants to go to the ball. And ... magic. Here comes the fairy godmother. Pumpkins, mice, glass slippers. No questions asked. Everything's fixed. Instantly.

Lovely. Lucky her. But life's not like that. I've lost count of how many times I've wished that it was. Most recently in the dark, black, heart-crushing moment when I realised that my depression was back. And just as awful as before. In that instant I would have given anything for a fairy godmother, or a magic wand, or a big red panic button that could provide a no-mess, no-fuss cure. Anything. Absolutely anything. I couldn't imagine ever finding the strength to pull myself out of the hole. Not again.

Yet now, I feel differently. Not because I'm well. If we're talking fairy tales, then I'm still not out of the woods. Not by a long way. The wolves are prowling. But, occasionally, I have a better day. Which feels like a miracle. And miracles are better than magic wands. Today, for the first time in well over a year, I was something approaching the mother that I want to be. All day. Even as I write this, I'm amazed. I didn't see it coming. I don't think anybody did.

It's days like today when I'm glad that there's no quick fix. Because, when the story ends, what did Cinderella learn from her adventure? That nothing changes without magic. And that shoes are amazing. I love magic, and fairy tales, and shoes. But

I can't build my life on them. No matter how hard I try. And I definitely don't want Elvie using that as her master plan. Tears, magic, prince. I like to think she'll hope for more.

These last few months have been difficult. Horribly difficult. Most of the time. But I can quite honestly say that if a fairy godmother showed up tomorrow with a magical 'quick fix' button, I wouldn't use it. At least, I don't think I would. I'm learning too much.

I'm learning that I have incredible friends. I've been honest and vulnerable and broken, and they haven't laughed in my face. Not once. They've picked me up and looked after me – and the children, and Wes. They've cheered me on and brought me cake and made me laugh when even the thought of laughing felt impossible.

I'm learning that I can write if I put my mind to it. That if I try hard enough, the words end up in the right order and that makes me happy. People even want to read them.

Most importantly, I'm learning that I am not alone. That there are so many others. Some have come through the other side. Some are lost in the woods right now, fighting their way through with their bare hands. Reading this and showing their faces. Holding out their hands, and taking the first steps towards recovery. There are no words for how that makes me feel. Privileged. Supported. And more than a little bit angry that we've all kept it hidden for so long.

I've worried that my children will grow up to be ashamed of me because of my depression. That I'll be an embarrassment. That they'll think I'm weak. Wes has never agreed. Thank goodness. He's convinced that they'll be proud of the fight and the bold and the facing-down-the-dragon-even-though-it's-scary. I'm starting to believe him. I'd rather be a real, honest, slightly battered role-model, muddling my way through with my family and friends than a shiny princess who has everything sorted out by a strange glittery pensioner with a wand. I'd rather my children know me as I am. So that they can learn to love themselves as they are. That's the plan, anyway.

I'm presuming that I get to keep the shoes.

All the water.

It's a 'morning-after-the-party-before' sort of day. Drinking tea, listening to the rain, eating leftovers and watching way more television than the health visitor recommends. Joel is alternating between sleeping and whinging. Exhausted by yesterday's frantic and successful attempts to flirt with every female guest. Elvie is dressed as a fairy. Sitting in a cardboard box.

Her toenails are still painted from yesterday. She did them herself. With poster paint. While everyone else was distracted. I've snuck off to the kitchen four times already, to eat handfuls of popping candy straight from the jar. And I'm prepared to award a knighthood to whoever invented the dishwasher. Mr Hotpoint, I presume. Thank you.

I'm shattered. We all are. Forty-five people in the garden for a barbecue, an astoundingly beautiful christening service, and the resulting hours of post-party clean-up would wear out even the strongest of souls. Thank goodness for grandparents who stay until ten o'clock to tidy. And children who are so tired that they pass out asleep at bedtime without so much as a murmur. For once.

I've been smiling all day. Despite the exhaustion and the incoming headache and the excessive popping candy consumption. Maybe not *despite* the popping candy. Sky-high sugar levels aside, the fact is that we did it. We actually did it. We got our children christened. We hosted a party. We had the downright cheek to ask people to celebrate with us. Even though I'm scared of hosting parties, and we only had paper plates and it was probably going to rain.

Guess what. It was wonderful. And it didn't even rain. People came. Everybody brought enough food. Nobody went hungry. Hardly anyone got paint on their clothes. Everyone smiled, and laughed, and mucked in. Friends loaned us bunting. Wes built a bench. Elvie's godfather arrived as we were serving dessert with all the necessary ingredients for Pimms. Perfect.

Admittedly, it wasn't professional. Not even slightly. Nothing matched, my attempt at a jelly in a mould was an unmitigated disaster, and there *may* have been some poo on the bathroom floor. But it was fun. So much fun that the children were ever so slightly late to their own christening service. Sorry, Rev.

Late or not, christened they were. Or baptised. Or splashed. Whatever. There was water, there was oil, and there were lots of tears. From both of them. Mostly Elvie. She was always high risk – there's a good reason that she never has showers.

It was only afterwards, with most of the tidying up finished and desperately needed mugs of tea in our hands, that my parents asked, 'So, why did you go for the water?' It's a fair question.

I've been part of various church communities for my entire life. But only recently have I joined one with a tradition of christening children. Full immersion adult baptism, yes. Dedications and thanksgivings for babies, absolutely. But christenings, with water? Not until now.

People have a lot of opinions. Every church I've joined has taken a different view. Some are sceptical of what they see as a magical attempt to win a place for your baby in heaven. Some think it's old-fashioned. Outdated. Some don't consider it a decision that you should make on your child's behalf. Some weren't particularly bothered either way. But either way, none of them did it. And so I grew up thinking that christenings were for Catholics. Or for keeping the grandparents happy. Or getting your child a space at an oversubscribed school.

And yet, yesterday, Elvie and Joel got wet. After a lot of soul-searching, and a decision that surprised everyone.

Even myself. Turns out I'm more traditional than I thought. It wasn't a magical attempt to secure them a spot in heaven. I'm pretty sure that's not how God works. It wasn't mystical or other-wordly. Not at all. The other children in the church filled the font with water, and they anointed my babies with oil. There was no smoke or mirrors. No big dresses, swinging incense or Latin words. Just puddles, noise and the most wonderful sense of community. Of love.

It was just us, our extended family and our incredible friends. Stepping into a tradition that has lasted for centuries. Welcoming our children into a church that crosses continents and generations and language barriers. A church that is more than delighted to have them.

It was, admittedly, a decision that we made on their behalf. But our days are riddled with those. Where we live. What we eat. When they go to bed. Where they play. Who they socialise with. What bedtime stories they read. What programmes they watch on television. I make those little decisions on their behalf every day. Often without thinking. Surely then, I should make the big decisions too. For now, at least. Guide them along the path, show them the way and hope that in time they pick it up as their own. That they feel as though it was always their own. That's the dream.

Perhaps it is a bit old fashioned. I know that not everyone agrees. That other people will dedicate their children. Or leave them to make their own decisions when they're older. Or have no opinion on the topic whatsoever and find it utterly incomprehensible that I've devoted so many words to something so irrelevant. But for us, and for our babies, it was right. Yesterday is a moment that I will cherish for the rest of my life. I knew that it would be lovely. Fun. Special. But I didn't expect it to be so precious. I didn't realise that it would take my breath away. Literally.

Some moments in time carry more weight than others.

Even the air feels heavier. The christening was one of those. From the moment we walked to the font, the hairs on my arms were standing to attention and I had to remind myself to breathe. The words that we spoke. The oil on their heads. The age-old prayers. Everyone standing together, by our sides, promising to care for our little ones. It's hard to put into words. It was more serious, more solemn and far more beautiful than I had ever expected.

We brought our two crazy, grubby bundles of quirk to God. Turns out He was very pleased to see them.

The one where nobody buys toddler milk.

I had a midlife crisis this afternoon. In Tesco.

Specifically, in the baby aisle. When Wes picked up two tubs of toddler formula instead of our usual baby milk. And my heart sank into my shoes.

I know the facts. In two weeks' time, my delicious little Joel will celebrate his first birthday. He'll officially be a toddler. I'm taking the complete-and-utter-denial approach to the matter. Which is working like a dream. Clearly.

The signs are everywhere. I tried to buy him some new shoes last week. From the baby section. Only to realise that none of the options were anywhere near strong enough for my boisterous, muddy, already-walking little boy. The mushed-up meals, fruit pots and biscuits that have filled our trolley for the last few months are now conspicuous in their absence. He's eating whatever we eat. It's frightening.

He's growing every day. He now has seven teeth, and size four feet. When you strap him into the buggy, he shouts 'Go!' Really loudly. And finds it hilarious. Last week he walked across an entire field with me, hand in hand. Like a proper little boy. This afternoon he paused, mid-bottle so that he could lean over for a kiss. He gets angry if I offer to help him. With anything. So I'm trying to step back. Mealtimes are messy.

I'm struggling to come to terms with it. The speed of it all. I put him to bed last night, and tried to slow down the minutes, determined to savour every last second. Curled up in the rocking chair with my warm, snuggly boy. Watching him fall asleep in my arms. It was beautiful. And fiercely bittersweet. These days are running out fast. He won't be a baby for long.

It was so much easier with Elvie. She was our first. I knew that there would be another baby. Maybe even a few. That I would have more chances to kiss little milky mouths, and cuddle cosy sleeping bundles. This time it's different. Joel is our last. And I can feel it. Like a physical pain in my chest.

I'm one of three children. As is Wes. I had always planned a house-full of babies – three, four, maybe even five. A home filled with busy and chaos and laughter sounds like perfection. To me, anyway. It's what I grew up with – my parents raised us whilst fostering, running a Sunday school and surrogate-parenting half of the church youth group. It wasn't unusual to find an unexpected guest at the breakfast table, having turned up overnight in distress. That's my baseline. My measuring stick. My emotional inheritance. I love it, and it's always been at the forefront of my dreams.

Dreams are lovely. Reality? That's a little trickier. Two bouts of postnatal depression are taking their toll. On me, on the children and on Wes. It's been tough on our marriage. Very tough. It's put the brakes on Wes's career. It's confused Elvie, and often it's left her distressed. Not to mention what has become of me and my state of mind. We're paying a very high price, and many times I've wondered if we'd make it through in one piece. Sometimes I still wonder. We can't take anything for granted.

Another baby would be a huge risk. Every single part of my brain knows that it would be a risk too far. I can't allow this black cloak to descend over my family for good. Over their lives and their happiness. Or mine. I know that. I really, truly do. It's just that my heart is a little more stubborn. The idea that our baby days are over, that these two brilliant, beautiful children are the only ones I'll ever have, is proving difficult to swallow. I know all the arguments, and I repeat them to myself. Over and over and over. But still my ridiculous heart whispers, 'Just one more.'

I don't know what to do. What are my options when I realise that I'm physically and emotionally incompatible with the dream that I've cherished for so many years? How do I carry on building a fulfilling life when in the back of my mind there is always someone missing? And how is it even possible to feel like this, when most days the two children I *do* already have are enough to make me drink gin from the bottle and be in bed by nine?

It's hard. It's painful. And it feels horribly selfish, when we have already been blessed with two healthy babies. I'm trying to focus on them. On the possibility that this way, I might be able to raise them more peacefully. That their home will (eventually) be a place of calm and consistency. That one day I might be able to parent in a way that doesn't leave me shot-through with guilt by bedtime. That depression may have won this battle, but that ultimately we, our little gang of four, will win the war.

I don't have the answers. But I put the toddler milk back this afternoon. One final act of denial. For old times' sake. I swapped it for baby formula. Just once more. I'm trying to make the most of my last baby, before he's all grown up. And I'll be staying away from Tesco for a while.

In which Elvie is a ripper.

We got off to a bad start this morning. It happens. Joel had a stinking cold, a grumpy face and a severe case of separation anxiety whenever Wes left the room. At which point Elvie inevitably decided that she too, just wanted Daddy. Despite admitting yesterday that Mummy is 'not too bad'. Thanks. Thanks a lot.

There was potential for this Daddy-centred day to work in my favour. A very tangible shot at a morning of drinking hot tea, reading books and getting things done. Providing of course, that Wes was around. Unfortunately, he left for work at 9.30. Leaving me with two grumpy babies who only wanted Daddy. There's nothing quite like children for boosting your self-esteem.

On days like this there's only one solution. For me, anyway. Get out. As soon as possible. Grumpy baby in the buggy. Elvie's shoes on. Changing bag packed. All ready for a trip into town to buy Joel some birthday presents. Perhaps he would have been a little less whingey if he'd known.

I carried out a last minute check in Elvie's room, to make sure there were no open windows, or juice bottles leaking onto the duvet covers. Instead, I found her Bible. The one that we bought for her christening, less than a month ago. The Bible I dragged the children into town to buy, and took so long choosing that the cashier despaired and gave up offering his advice. The Bible that Wes and I sat with for hours, despite our zombie-like state of exhaustion, trying to write a suitably poignant message inside. One that would convey all our parental emotions on such an auspicious day. The Bible that I had hoped she would cherish and love and pass down to her own children one day.

It was lying in the middle of her bedroom floor. Ripped to pieces. I'm pretty sure that people have been burnt at the stake for less. I resisted that temptation. Much too messy. Instead, I removed it from her room, with the promise that I'd take away all her other books as well if she insisted on ripping them. Which is much more reasonable. And a lot less burny.

This isn't the first book she's ripped. There's a pile of

them on my shelf, waiting to be fixed. It drives me crazy. And it's not just books. She pulls her toys to pieces, picks all the sparkles off her dress-up clothes and one day, when she was really bored, she ripped up every single piece of her favourite farmyard jigsaw puzzle. And carried them all into the kitchen to show me. Pleased as punch.

All this wanton destruction makes me cross. But mostly, it makes me sad. Really sad. I've always had strong attachments to objects, even as a child. I still have the bear I received on my first birthday, worn and battered and missing an ear. I've fallen in love with ugly daisies and old knitted toys. I gave stories to everything I found, and developed very emotional ties to some pretty unorthodox items.

These days I'm better at looking at things rationally. Throwing things out. I even have an entirely impractical desire for the minimalist spaces that show up every week on *Grand Designs*. I recently implemented 'Operation Clean-up' in an attempt to reclaim our house from the clutter that is currently colonising every available surface. It's a painfully slow process but if I've given it a name, it's totally going to happen.

Despite my new-found ruthlessness, there is one area in which I am still a chronically sentimental hoarder. Unfortunately it's fairly all-encompassing. Broadly speaking it's filed under anything-that-has-a-memory-attached-to-it-or-could-one-day-be-used-to-make-something-beautiful. I have boxes of buttons, fabric scraps and art equipment, as well as every letter, memento and card that I've received in the last fifteen years. I've kept every picture Elvie has ever drawn. I've got bags of the children's cutest baby clothes, with a view to turning them into keepsake blankets. At some point. I've got baby books for both of them, in varying stages of completion, notebooks for writing down funny things they say and shoeboxes full of ticket stubs, newspaper clippings and christening cards. Not to mention the photos.

It seems that I have an inbuilt desire to preserve everything. Clearly I've missed my vocation as a museum curator. I spend many happy hours daydreaming about the scrapbooks I'll make for my children when they grow up. To be presented on their eighteenth birthdays. Or some other suitably meaningful occasion. I'm hoping they'll give them an insight into their childhood. Show them how very loved they have always been. And obviously, provide the opportunity for rapturous appreciation of my foresight and skill at managing to save everything and present it all so beautifully.

This borderline fanatical desire for preservation makes it tough to deal with Elvie in full-on wrecking mode. Especially when she destroys things that I've put thought and effort into, and desperately hoped she would love. Like her Bible. I can't help but take it all personally.

I know. She's three years old. As of last week. Perhaps she'll grow into her emotional attachments. Or maybe she'll always hold things lightly. Maybe I'll present her with a truckload of scrapbooks and baby blankets on her twenty first birthday, and she'll smile politely and send them straight to storage.

I need to embrace the fact that, despite our similarities, she's not actually me. That she works differently. I can't spend the rest of my life fighting it. I don't have the energy. I need to accept that the recording and remembering and commemorating is just as much for my benefit as it is for hers. So that I can remember the good times. Cherish them. And hopefully get better at noticing them whilst they're happening. I need to remember that often, she rips things to pieces when she's bored. Or angry. That perhaps we need some new strategies for dealing with complex emotions.

We managed to salvage today. After hours of hunting for the perfect, reasonably-priced toy car, Joel fell asleep in the buggy. So Elvie and I shared a treat. Pancakes, juice and an entertaining game of guess-what-random-name-the-Starbucks-lady-will-write-on-our-cup-today.

Maybe one day the story of her Bible-ripping will make it into her scrapbook. We'll look back and laugh, amazed at how far we've come. Hopefully. Until then, it has joined the other damaged books on the shelf. If only for my own sanity. She won't be seeing that again for a while.

Telling your story with cake.

Last night I had dinner with two of my very favourite girlfriends. Today Joel was so poorly that we ended up in A&E. Last night I drank red wine and ate squishy raspberry meringue. Today I googled mysterious rashes and tried to cool down my delirious, rambling baby. Last night I was happy. Today I was afraid.

Joel will be fine. Apparently a viral throat infection, teething and an unexpected allergic reaction are a less-than-desirable combination. By bedtime he was suitably medicated, throwing food out of his highchair and racing up the stairs. Normal service is slowly being resumed.

As the panic subsides, I can look back on the last twenty-four hours in amazement. Happiness? Fear? Those sound an awful lot like feelings. Emotions. Actual real emotions. That I felt. In the moment. That don't look grey, or numb, or washed out. Which is odd.

The last few months have turned me into something of an expert at numbing. With a minor in poorly-concealed anger. That's how my depression manifests itself. As an all-consuming numbness. It's a way of coping. Of shutting myself off. Protecting myself. At least, that's how it feels. Initially. Eventually it reveals itself as a trap. A dirty great grey-walled prison. Finally I'm beginning to understand why.

On a friend's recommendation, I've been reading Brené Brown's extraordinary research that mostly deals with shame and imperfection. And is way more fun than it sounds. According to her studies, it is scientifically impossible to engage in selective numbing. Which means that, no matter how hard I try to beat the system, numbing away pain also wipes out beauty. So that I end up feeling nothing. At all.

I don't understand the science. Brain chemistry is not my area of expertise. But I'm living proof that her findings are true. Her words are a revelation. Not so much for Wes, admittedly, who's been trying to make exactly the same point for months now. I always get there in the end.

It's shining a light on a lot of my quirks. Like the way that I play down any positive occurrences. As if admitting the possibility of future happiness is somehow asking for trouble. Setting myself up for a fall of epic proportions. I certainly daren't tempt fate by getting excited about upcoming events. I'm much more comfortable worrying about the logistics, or fretting about the extra hassle.

Hard though it is to admit, I've become afraid of fun. I can't quite face being happy. It feels like too much of a risk. Too far removed from my safe, comfortable, suffocating grey. So much so that, nine months after Wes bought me *Matilda* tickets for my birthday, we still haven't seen it. I've not even booked our seats.

It turns out that it's important to tell your story. To face it head-on. All of it. Even the hard parts. If I'm not telling it deliberately, with words or art, or communication of some kind, I'll numb it away. At least that's what Dr Brown suggests. And I believe her. I know that feeling. I know those days. The days when everything feels too hard. Too hard to talk about, or write about. Too hard to think about. Those are the days when I curl up in a blanket. When the words don't come. When I tell my story with cake, crappy telly and hours of aimless Facebook stalking. Numbing my emotions away. Controlling what I let myself feel, and what I don't. Never actually dealing with any of it.

And then, in the final giveaway of my numbed-out state,

I stop creating. Creativity is vulnerable. It's risky. However it's expressed. Baking, writing, painting, gardening, or joining in when your children sing show tunes in the street. For instance. To create is to take a chance. To put a little piece of yourself out into the world. Open to criticism. And people's interpretations. Numb is easier. By far.

Elvie's creativity is amazing. Completely unfettered. Inspiring. Most of the time, I love it. But when I'm depressed, I try to numb her too. Stop jumping. Be quiet. Stop asking questions. No more stories. Would you please just keep the clothes on your Sylvanian rabbits for five godforsaken minutes? She resists. Understandably. I would, if anyone was trying to suck the colour out of *my* world.

She's resilient. I'll give her that. It takes approximately twenty eight seconds for her to forget that I was trying to slow her down. By which point she's already creeping away from the imaginary giant in her latest game. Whatever disappointment her day brings, I can guarantee that she doesn't go to bed at night wishing she could stay there for the rest of the week.

I'm trying to follow her lead. To defrost. Get my feelings back. To tell my story with words or creativity rather than cake and telly and Facebook. I'm trying to share more. To talk more. Even on the hard days. To take some risks. Maybe I'll even book *Matilda* tickets. Life on the edge, people. Right here.

Letting your feelings back in can be hard. This afternoon I was so worried about Joel that my body shut down and I went utterly, completely blank for half an hour. Switching off. Trying to cope with the scared and the not-knowing.

It's like pins and needles. In my brain. Numb and cold and then, in an instant, incredibly uncomfortable. With precious little warning. At least with pins and needles, the pain goes away. Eventually. And you can move your limbs again.

Does it work the same for emotions? Who knows?

Fingers crossed.

AUTUMN

September

One of them.

Today we celebrated Joel's very first birthday. In all the traditional ways. Presents? Check. Cards? Of course. Ice cream? Naturally. First, terrifying dose of antidepressants? What? No? Just me then.

The last few weeks have been brutal. Evidently. The summer holidays stole away my carefully crafted routine, and all our toddler group sanctuaries. Wes has alternated between being away or working all of the hours, every day. Elvie has been bored. And Joel has been scarily ill with what turned out not to be measles after all. We've had a lot on our plates. And it hasn't all been birthday cake.

Wes was home at the weekend. Just for a few hours. Between jobs. Somewhat unwisely, given our mutual exhaustion levels, we attempted to embark on a serious conversation. It took all of seven minutes to become a fully-fledged, screaming, sobbing argument. On my part, anyway. We argued about how much he works. How often he's away. How powerless I feel, being left behind to cope. How there's no way he could ever understand. How I never get a say in any of it. Not really.

The stripped-down, bare-bones facts of the matter are these: if he works, I can't cope. If he doesn't work, we don't eat.

There are no easy answers. None. We've tried. Believe me.

With that in mind, I called my doctor this morning. He

saw me straight away. He thinks the drugs are a step in the right direction. I wish I could be so certain.

There's only one thing I know for sure; we can't carry on like this. I've been using Wes as my antidepressant. When he's around, life feels more manageable. The children frustrate me less. I can keep my head above water. Or on my pillow at least. When he's away, it's all too much. And everyone suffers. It's not fair on any of us. Something has to change and it seems that, despite my best efforts, that something needs to be me.

There are no words to adequately express how annoying this is. Seriously. I've been doing everything right. I'm talking to people. I'm writing. I'm following my therapy programme, albeit not as quickly as they would like. I'm reading inspiring books. I'm getting out of the house nearly every day. I'm a textbook candidate for a full and speedy recovery. And yet. Nothing.

I've always believed that if you work hard enough, and you try your best, everything turns out right. Well. Not this time.

To top it off, I have an irrational fear of medication. Not the actual tablet-swallowing, but the consequences. The side effects. I took the pill for six months and felt as though I'd actually lost my mind. Wes has to convince me to take Nurofen if I have a migraine. Even then, I'd rather not. In labour with Joel, a year ago today, I made it to the final pushing stage on two paracetamol and a bag of jelly babies. But now?

Now I am 'one of them'.

The ones who need tablets to survive. Who tick the 'Yes actually, I am taking other medication' box on all the forms. Who turn down the alcohol they would so dearly love because Fluoxetine is not a good mixer. Part of the infamous 'Prozac Nation' that the 1990s held so dear.

And I'm scared. Really scared.

Scared of the endless list of potential side effects that

everyone told me not to read. Scared that I'll never be in a position to wean myself off. Scared of becoming dependent, a pill-popping junkie, despite the sworn assurances of my doctor that it's not even a possibility. Not on these drugs, anyway. Mostly, I'm scared that I'll disappear inside myself. That I won't know who I am anymore. What's me, and what's the tablets talking.

Also, I'm embarrassed. Mortified. At being one of those people who just can't cope by themselves. One of them. I've always managed anything I turned my hand to. So long as I wanted it badly enough, and it didn't involve too many numbers.

But I can't do *this*. Not by myself. I need help. Which is the toughest thing I've ever had to admit. To write. I almost didn't. Write it, that is. Wondering if it would be just a bit too much honesty. A little too warts-and-all. A teeny-tiny step beyond the point of no-return. Or maybe a leap.

And yet. Sometimes you just have to swallow your pride, and your tablets, and confess that you're only human. Apparently this is one of those times.

I must have looked stunned when the doctor agreed so quickly to my tentative suggestion of medication, because he just gave me his all-knowing smile and asked, 'If you'd broken your arm, would you want me to put it in plaster or just leave it hanging around?' He has a point. As usual. It's just that a broken arm would be easier. People can see that. It looks real. It's a lot less likely to be dismissed as a self-indulgent misery-fest.

I can't figure out how I feel. It's all a bit of a muddle. All I know is that I didn't take my prescription to our local pharmacy. Just in case someone saw me. In case I went down in the estimation of the lovely lady behind the counter. Who normally sells me Calpol, or nit lotion, or plasters. Instead I went into town. To the biggest chemist I could find, in an attempt to be anonymous. For a little while, at least.

I realised two things as I waited in line for my

prescription. Sandwiched in amongst the old ladies waiting for their osteoporosis tablets, the heroin addicts taking their methodone and the chatty teenager who reliably informed me that she was also there for antidepressants. Firstly, not all pharmacists are as concerned with patient confidentiality as you might wish. Clearly. And secondly, I can't get up on my high horse if you judge me. For needing the pills. For taking them. For being unable to cope. Until this morning, I would have judged me too.

I'm not sure I agree that everything happens for a reason. But I'm a definite fan of dragging something good out of a crisis. Kicking and screaming, if need be. And no matter what happens over the next few months or years, or however long I'm taking these pills, I will never be the same. Neither will my view of the world. Or the people in it.

Because, in reality, we're all 'one of them'. 'They' are, in fact, us. I know that now. Some of us just hide it better than others.

New names. And tomatoes.

Something beautiful is happening in my garden. There's a tomato. And it's growing. An actual real-life tomato. The best part? I grew it. By myself. From a tiny seed. Like an actual real-life gardener.

Back in April, I channelled my inner Felicity Kendal and decided to try growing things. (In related information, I'd just added my name to the council's allotment waiting list in a rush of over-enthusiasm after a single session of toddler gardening club, and I figured I could probably use the practice.)

Growing a tomato is a big deal. For me, anyway. I'm very much a novice. So much so that I used upturned plastic cutlery to label my pots and had no idea what strain of tomatoes we were growing. I still don't. They're definitely medium-sized. If that helps.

I'm well aware that summer is officially over, and that we will be eating green tomato chutney for the next four years if the rest of the fruits don't hurry up and ripen. I accept that my strawberries have been eaten from the inside out by some tiny, mysterious bugs. I am fully aware that our sunflowers were shorter than my three year old. It wouldn't pass for a successful summer on most plots.

Nonetheless, there is a shiny red tomato growing in my garden. And it's there because I grew it. I planted it. I watered it. Most of the time. I palmed it off on our neighbour when we went away. And look what happened. Look what I did. It's amazing.

Perhaps you are a natural gardener. Blessed with green fingers and good soil. Or even the ability to recognise good soil when you see it. Me? I can kill anything. Flowers, herbs, vegetables. You name it, I've killed them all. Remember the 'air plants' from the 1990s that were glued to pieces of wood and only needed an occasional misting? I've even killed those, and I'm eighty per cent certain they're immortal.

It's become a standing joke and, as so often happens, I've adopted it as part of my story. Mother, wife, daughter, plant-killer. You know the drill.

Except that I'm not a plant-killer. Not anymore. I'm a plant grower. A vegetable grower, no less. With a tomato to prove it. I should probably get some proper wellies.

That lonely red tomato, and the children's gardening club, are helping me to rethink my story. To change how I look at myself, what I call myself, and who I think I am. So are the tablets. That's the master plan, after all. That they change the way I see the world. But they're changing me in other ways too.

I tell a lot of stories about myself, when I'm alone. I

call myself all sorts of names when nobody else can hear. Names that I'd never dream of using on anyone else. For as long as I can remember, the overarching theme of my secret narrative has been that I am not quite 'good enough'. I've been a closet perfectionist, searching for that elusive picture-postcard family, or outfit or interior design scheme. Scraping my way through. Hoping that I'd maintain sufficient control to impress everyone. Waiting to be found out.

Unsurprisingly, it hasn't brought me much joy. It hasn't brought me much of anything, in fact. The pressure of hunting perfection can really slow you down. Even when the pressure is only coming from yourself. Everything I love has been squashed into the background, suffocating under a mountain of 'trying-desperately-to-be-good-enough.' The reality is that I don't much care about hoovering, or pattern matching, or behaving in an entirely respectable manner. Ask anyone I've ever lived with.

And yet I've still been striving. Striving towards perfection, along with the approval-of-others and self-satisfaction that I hoped would follow. Repeating the pattern that started years ago, when a relentlessly academic all-girls Oxbridge-feeding grammar school taught me that creativity and non-conformity were categorically unacceptable. But that everyone would love you if you got good grades, kept it together and didn't fall over at prize giving.

I've chased that story for almost twenty years. I've had my moments of glorious Technicolor, university-avoiding, drama-school rebellion. And I've loved them. But I've always returned to 'not good enough.' By whose standards? I'm not sure.

It's almost a relief to realise that actually, the good ship Perfect set sail long ago. And I've missed it. Well and truly. For now I'm swallowing my pills and working through my depression and wondering if I needed to get so thoroughly blown off course in order to realise that I had been steering in the wrong direction all along.

All the parts of my nature that I've fought in my quest for perfection, are all the parts that I most love. That bring me joy. That intrigue me. Or scare me. That make me feel alive.

So I'm trying to change my story. Change the way I think about myself, and the names I call myself when nobody's listening. It's not entirely out of choice. I've been rumbled. I've failed. Perhaps that's no bad thing.

No longer will I be mother, wife, daughter, plant-killer, perfection-hunter, who's-not-quite-good-enough-at-anything-useful.

I'm aiming for mother, wife, daughter, creative, truth-teller, lover-of-beautiful-things, creator-of-beautiful-things, messy-and-learning-and-working-at-being-ok-with-that.

It's long. No denying that. It won't fit on a name badge. But I think I'm okay with that too.

Seasons.

On Thursday evening I made dinner whilst looking out at the garden and admiring summer. It felt as though it had settled in. Taken root. Like it had been around for so long that it might just last forever.

On Friday morning it was raining and the temperature had dropped by almost ten degrees.

Autumn arrived overnight. Literally. Even the air smells different. Bonfires and blankets and *Strictly Come Dancing*. We're all wearing socks. And jumpers. And we all have colds already.

Every year, without fail, I'm surprised by autumn. Usually it just sneaks in, creeping up on the end of another miserable, wet summer. But this year, someone flicked a switch. I suspect I'm not the only one that got caught out.

We've had unbelievable weather this summer. The kind that makes emigrating seem much less essential. I can't remember the last time we had such a long run of glorious, unbroken sunshine. Or the last time we used this much sun cream. There've been so many angry demands for ice lollies. So many entirely futile requests for the children to wear their hats, or to play in the shade. This year I'm ready for crisp and cold and cosy – so long as it comes with plenty of fairy lights and a good warm helping of crumble.

Seasons are magical. The knowing-what's-coming-and-yet-still-being-surprised. Such huge changes within such a predictable rhythm. Four chances every year to start over, with the reassurance that, whatever happens, there will always be a next time. Wes grew up in South Africa and I'm always amazed that he survived eighteen years without summer drifting into autumn, and winter melting into spring. I don't think I could do it.

There are new seasons a-plenty in our house right now. Elvie starts nursery on Friday. Joel strides a little further from babyhood every single day. Wes has more work than ever. And I'm stepping up the seemingly endless battle against my depression. With a little help from the pharmacy.

I've been wary of people who talk about the seasons in their lives. It's always sounded a bit airy-fairy. Hippies and woollen clothes and tambourines. But right now, it makes sense. In the space of a fortnight, everything is changed. All within the constant, predictable rhythm of our everyday lives. From the outside everything looks the same. But inside, things are changing. Even the air smells different. Like hope. And cough medicine.

Our change has been just as sudden as the change in the weather. And it's taken us equally by surprise. September is only nine days old, and already it's packed full of beautiful memories. Children dancing until midnight at weddings, singing nursery rhymes under frosty countryside stars, birthday cakes and candles and little walking feet.

Seasons don't last forever. That's not how they work. But we're crossing our fingers that we cling onto this one for a while.

Big questions for little people.

I love blogs. I can spend hours reading them. Clicking link after link after link, until I realise that whole evenings have passed. Poking my nose into other people's homes, lives and parenting strategies. Especially their parenting strategies. I'm stunned by the conversations these people have with their children. The inspired, brilliant ways that they tackle the deep, emotional issues. And the responses from their children. Who actually seem to listen.

I've been taking notes. On the premise that I have time to plan my tactics when it comes to the big questions – God, faith, death. You know the ones. After all, preschoolers don't deal in abstract concepts. Not yet. Right? Hmmm. About that.

Recently we visited my parents, just for the day. True to form, Elvie didn't want to leave, and so she hid. Eventually I found her. Completely naked, giggling and plastered in wet sand. Under their bedcovers. That sheet's going to need a wash.

As I bundled her downstairs she spotted a photo of a baby and naturally assumed that it was her. She was a little put out to discover that it was in fact, Aunty Melany. Until she realised that she'd never heard that name before. And out came the questions. Where is Melany? Where did she grow up?

I was blindsided. Caught completely off guard, with no time to craft a carefully worded response. So I told her the truth.

I told her that Melany didn't grow up. That she died when she was only a baby. That she was very poorly, and she had a hole in her heart that couldn't be fixed, and that everyone is still very sad about it. Especially Grandma.

Elvie sat for a while. Scraping the sand off her knees. Taking everything in. Whilst I pondered the dubious wisdom of being entirely honest with an only-just-three-year-old. More questions. Where is she now? Will she ever come back? What does she do in heaven?

I answered her as truthfully as I could. Go honest, or go home. Or something. She got up and wandered off to find her previously abandoned clothes. She seemed satisfied. And I assumed the conversation was over.

Like many three year olds, Elvie loves playing doctors. Her medical bag is her most precious possession. That and her ballet dress. As a result, I spend several hours each week attending to the minor ailments of a selection of soft toys.

Elvie always plays their mother. Bringing them into my surgery with a concerned look on her face. Skipping off happily when they are better. Promising to return soon with 'another problem.' She loves it. I'm beginning to think she has Munchausen by Proxy. Which is the only thing I ever learnt from *ER*.

This week there has been a recurring condition amongst my cuddly patients. They all have holes in their hearts. 'Like baby Melany.' Turns out the conversation isn't over, after all.

It's impossible to know if I've done the right thing. It's certainly not as clear cut as those bloggers make it look. I worry about a three year old grappling with life's big questions. Issues that people twenty times her age struggle to understand. I don't want life, or death, weighing heavy on her little shoulders.

Equally, I don't want to lie. Or hide anything. I love the idea of being completely honest, in an age-appropriate way. It's just that I have no way of knowing what's going on in that busy head of hers. Whether it's all too much, too soon.

This morning we were at our usual Wednesday toddler group. Relishing the start of term, and the return of our routine. Over tea and biscuits talk turned to one of their former volunteers, who had died earlier in the year. Never one to be left out, Elvie came to join the conversation. Needless to say, she had some questions.

We explained that the lady had died. Of a poorly heart. Elvie nodded. This was familiar territory now. Did she go to heaven? Yes. Like baby Melany? Yes.

More sitting. More thinking. So much goes on inside that brain. In the end I asked a question ... 'What do you think they're doing in heaven?'

Elvie thought for a minute. And smiled.

'I think they're at ballet school.'

And that's how I knew we were okay. For now, at least. Nothing but nothing on earth could be better, in Elvie's eyes, than ballet school. Unless there was a ballet school where you could wear a stethoscope. That might just clinch it.

It will be years before she feels the sadness of it all. Of any of it. And that's absolutely fine. That's how it should be. Somehow the photo and our little chats and the endless cycle of stuffed-toy-doctor-appointments have turned a concept that's new and scary and hard into something that she knows. Something she can deal with.

I wish that I'd had time to think over my answers. Just a little bit of warning. A chance to skim back over a few of my favourite blogs and compare notes. In reality, I'm starting to realise that I won't ever get that luxury. Whatever the issue – death, sex, body piercings – I expect that I will always be caught unawares.

The conversation will never be over. And I will never be prepared. In which case, honest might just be the way to go.

Red gates.

We're two weeks into our brand new routine, and I've decided. I like being a nursery mum. I like it a lot. Mostly because it's 1.15 p.m. and I'm sitting on the sofa, writing. By myself. Joel is asleep in his cot and Elvie, if our lunchtime chat was anything to go by, is currently playing tricks on her teachers in an attempt to get onto the much-coveted 'amber face'. Which was probably not the desired effect of this discipline system.

I have time to myself. In the day. For the first time in nearly two years. It's so quiet. I can drink a whole cup of tea, or read an entire article, or pay the gas bill over the phone without the automated system throwing me out repeatedly because Joel's screams don't match our postcode. All those little luxuries.

I'm struggling to get my head around the fact that my baby girl is old enough for nursery. That she's spending fifteen hours a week in someone else's care. We've been joined at the hip for three years and now, finally, we have some breathing space. Just in time.

Admittedly she isn't far away. This afternoon I could hear her singing in the playground from the comfort of my lounge. With the windows closed. But it's a big step, for both of us.

For Elvie, it's a chance at some independence. For the intellectual stimulation that she so desperately craves, that she can't get at home with Mummy and a baby brother. It's an opportunity to venture out by herself into the big wide world. They even have a slide. It doesn't get better than that.

For me it's a first glimpse of the fact that time does,

eventually, move on. That things *will* change. That I won't be stuck at home with two very demanding tinies forever. No matter how life feels right now. There have been many, many times when I thought this day would never come. The fact that it arrived at all is enough to knock me sideways with gratitude. No matter how it goes.

Thankfully, it's going well. It has been from the very first day when Elvie walked straight in, hung up her coat and only looked back for long enough to ask us to leave. Three years old, and already we're cramping her style. When I picked her up, she was beaming. By the time we'd made the three minute walk home, she had informed me that she'd had 'tremendous' fun with her new friends, that she couldn't remember any of their names, and that she couldn't wait to go back. It's possible that my joyful shout of relief was slightly louder than I intended.

It's amazing what a bit of space can do. Every time I drop her off, I feel a swell of pride. Watching her, so confident, bombing around with her new friends. Barely even turning around to say goodbye. At home time when she runs at me, waving a letter about the latest contagious disease that's sweeping the school, I'm genuinely pleased to see her. Which makes a nice change.

Seven years ago I was a drama student. Studying at the school I'd always dreamed of, and still in a state of utter disbelief at having been accepted. Every morning, as I walked up the steps, engraved with the names of its most famous alumni, I would pinch myself as I realised that my dreams were coming true. Unless it was raining. In which case I put my head down and ran straight to the canteen for a cup of tea and a Mars bar.

Strange as it may seem, the nursery gates are my new drama-school steps. There's nothing carved into them except graffiti, and there's no chance of a hot drink or a snack.

They're red painted monstrosities with an automatic timer that locks you out if you're late. Apparently. But they serve the same purpose. Every day, when I walk through those gates I'm reminded that my biggest dream, for most of my life, has been to have a family of my own. And here they are. Right in front of me.

The first years of parenting are breathtakingly intense. And depression has stolen a lot of the joy that usually helps balance that out. It's hard to be grateful when you barely have the energy to lift your head off the pillow.

Nursery has given me that breathing space. The opportunity to stand back and see what's really going on. To wait at the gates. To see my children from the outside for a little while. And I'm so very thankful.

Working Girl.

This week heralds the start of a brave new era. Wes and I went away for twenty four precious hours. By ourselves. No children. To a hotel. In what Wes likes to refer to as 'up north,' but is in fact Leicestershire.

For most couples, the first night away post-children means a massage, a leisurely dinner in a fancy restaurant and an early night (nudge nudge, wink wink). Followed by reading the papers over a room service breakfast in the morning. It would appear that we are not most couples.

Our twenty four hours away consisted of a dash to Tesco for snacks, a hasty but delicious pizza in the bar, 300 photos of half-naked men, manoeuvring our combined body weight in photography equipment through hotel corridors and appeasing mildly inebriated middle-aged women. Before collapsing into bed at 2 a.m., sleeping way past breakfast and stopping at Wetherspoons for a fry-up on the way home.

Oh yes. This week, I went to work with Wes. And it was fabulous.

Wes has many strings to his professional bow, one of which involves running photobooths at corporate parties. Taking photos of slightly intoxicated guests draping themselves over scantily clad male models, and then printing out all the pictures so that everyone has a nice folder to take home at the end of the evening as a memento. It's a ridiculous amount of fun.

This week it was the turn of the fragrance counter employees of a national department store. And I was the photographer's assistant. Which meant that I spent the night running from the party – where Wes was taking the pictures - to the green room, where I was printing them out. And back again. And again. And again. In heels. Swapping memory cards and ink cartridges and restraining myself from adjusting the colour settings on the printers to reduce the intensity of the fake tan on display. All whilst attempting to breathe in a building where the air was ninety per cent perfume.

It was brilliant. Yes, by the time I went to bed I'd been awake for twenty three hours straight. Yes, spending the evening in a room full of dancers gives you quite an inferiority complex. And yes, being in charge of a table covered in technology is not my strongest suit. But we were fine. In fact, we did a great job.

Truth is, it all felt very familiar. It was the closest I've been to the theatre since my drama school days. Wearing blacks and sneaking around backstage. Bright lights, loud music and girls being sewn into costumes. Tins of sweets, bottles of water and inside information about reality television pay-scales. The instant sense of community that comes from a group of strangers working hard and loving what they do. Even at 2 a.m.

I hadn't realised how much I miss that buzz. That feeling

of being on the inside. Part of something. Part of a team. Motherhood can be a lonely business.

I see other people. Of course I do. At toddler groups, in the park, or at the nursery gates. We compare stories. Commiserating over our broken sleep or our vomiting children or the fact that it's only a week into term and we've already had letters home about head lice, chicken pox and scarlet fever.

But, for the majority of my day as a stay-at-home-mum, I'm on my own. Making lunch, getting the baby to nap, finding shoes, hanging washing, giving the dolls a tea party, making dinner, wiping grubby faces, doing nursery runs, changing nappies, clearing toys. Over and over again. Wes is supportive, but he's not always here. Most of the time it's just me. And the children.

Which is hard. Really hard. Especially when it transpires that some grown-up chat, the sound of a distant bass and a few sequins help me to feel alive. I can't see a way round it. Unless we move to a commune, and quite frankly, tie-dye is not my favourite. The truth is, this is just a phase. I know that. It won't last forever. It's a lonely phase, no question, but I need to find a way to live in it, as best I can, instead of wishing it away. Whilst staying as sane as possible. The occasional night off – work-related or otherwise – might just help.

In the interests of sanity (and my ever-expanding free fragrance collection), I have offered to reprise my role as photographer's assistant, should the opportunity present itself. My offer has been accepted. Who knows, maybe next time we'll even manage a massage.

October

Not all mental patients have chainsaws.

Here's the thing.

I am a mental patient.

I take my tablets, as prescribed, every single day. I have fortnightly therapy sessions, and a computerised, robot-voiced CBT course to keep me company in between. 'He-llo Ha-nnah.'

All of them trying to calm the chaos inside my head. To pull me back to a place where I can function properly. A place where I can be happy.

It's taken me a long time to admit that I'm ill. Too long. Years. Partly because it doesn't fit the image that I want to project. Partly because I always felt like I *should* be able to cope by myself. But mostly because it's not something that people talk about.

No wonder.

This morning we went to the corner shop for a loaf of bread. In between six-point-turning the buggy through the only-just-wide-enough door, and stopping Elvie scootering into the cakes, I caught a glimpse of the newspapers. Just the top of the *Sun*'s headline. '1200 KILLED.'

I racked my brains. I lost most of my weekend to man flu, chocolate pudding and *Strictly*, but I'm sure I would have noticed a natural disaster or an act of terrorism. If only because there was a link to it on Facebook. I bought the bread, avoided any further cake-related carnage and eventually succumbed to my curiosity. I read the front page, and regretted it immediately.

'1200 KILLED BY MENTAL PATIENTS.' Bright red numbers. Capital letters.

Angry doesn't quite cover it. My blood was boiling. No wonder we keep our conditions to ourselves. No wonder we hide away. Convinced that we're monsters. No wonder Asda thought it appropriate to sell 'mental patient' outfits for Halloween. We're an easy target.

It doesn't take much courage to go after the quiet ones. The ones who don't stand up for themselves. Because they have been shamed into silence. It's weak. It's cowardly. And it's really unfair.

There is some truth behind the headline. A friend who works in the NHS sent me a copy of the report that they're quoting. The *National Confidential Inquiry into Suicide and Homicide by People with Mental Illness*, published by the University of Manchester, in July 2013. And they're right. Over the last decade 1200 people have been killed by individuals who were receiving treatment for mental illness. Which is horrendous. 1200 families ripped apart. 1200 tragedies that could possibly have been avoided. Horrible. Heartbreaking. Tragic.

My issue is with the reporting. The generalising and the scaremongering. The fact that they took a study intended to improve the care and safety of mental patients, and used it to turn those same individuals into objects of fear. The fact is that, as a percentage, the number of mentally ill people committing homicide is no higher than that of any other randomly selected focus group. There are statistics for that as well. They neglected to mention those. Because they won't sell papers.

'Mental patients.' That sells. Cuckoos' nests. Jekyll and Hyde. Uncontrollable. High on prescription drugs. Dealing with our multiple personalities or schizophrenia or depression, whilst living on your street. Hiding in amongst the 'normal people'. Just waiting to whip out our chainsaws at the first hint of a full moon.

Has anyone counted the number of homicides committed by cancer patients in the last decade? What about asthmatics? I doubt whether the *Sun* would be so fascinated by a report on crime rates amongst the diabetic community. Mental illness doesn't attract the same sympathy. Because we're scary. Different. Broken. Dangerous.

It's true. 1200 people is an awful total. But over the same period of time, according to exactly the same report, over 13,000 mental patients have taken their own lives. More than ten times as many. Unable to deal with the stigma. The shame. The fear. The overwhelming, exhausting brutality of fighting your own mind. Day in, day out.

The *Sun* decided to ignore that. And they're paying for it already. Outrage. Finally. On our behalf. Because the simple truth is this: we're no more broken or dangerous than anybody else. No matter what the tabloids would have you believe.

I am a mental patient. But I'm also a wife, a mother, a daughter, a sister and a friend. I collect recipe books, and buttons. I make incredible roast potatoes. I had a very brief career as a stiltwalker. I could happily spend days on end curled up under a blanket watching *Strictly*. I can't wait for the cold weather so that I can wear my boots again. I sincerely believe that most of the world's problems could be solved by a nice cup of tea and a chat. I adore vintage fairground rides. Just the thought of Christmas makes me smile.

Nobody can be summed up in one paragraph. Certainly not in one sentence, and absolutely not in two words. 'Mental patients' are people too. Real people. I promise.

We already face huge challenges. We're already being as brave as we possibly can. Too many of us are disappearing. Unable to face our friends and family. Unable to face ourselves.

It's time to start telling our stories. Stories that draw on trust and hope and empathy. Rather than cementing our fears and prejudices. Focusing on the things that bring communities together. Not what pulls us apart. That's the only way things will get better.

It might not sell many papers. That's fine by me.

Then again, I am mental.

Who is this Lelli Kelly anyway?

Today is International Day of the Girl. Celebrating every girl's right to education and wellbeing. Pressing for an end to forced marriage and FGM. One step closer to gender equality. How did Elvie celebrate? By filling her treasure box with imaginary make-up and deciding that 'being pretty' was the most important quality in any potential friend.

Not the proudest moment of my parenting journey thus far.

I know exactly who to blame. Lelli Kelly. If that is her real name. Advertising her beautiful sparkly shoes and their accompanying cosmetic compacts, all over toddler television. Ten year old girls, styled to within an inch of their lives, giggling and twirling in sequin-encrusted ballet pumps that cost nearly as much as our mortgage.

Elvie has seen that advert twice. Maybe three times. And yet at dinner time last night she told me that she likes the Lelli Kelly girls. Because they're so pretty. That she thinks she needs some make-up. So that she can be a bit more beautiful. I hear her singing, 'Lelli Kelly, Lelli Kelly,' to herself as she dances round the kitchen. And it breaks my heart.

I have a longstanding suspicion of rhyming names. That cutesy veneer must be hiding something. Dora the Explorer? Persistent tweenage runaway with a penchant for illegal exotic pets. Dennis the Menace? That's a life of crime just waiting to happen. And now Lelli Kelly. Flogging body-confidence issues to pre-schoolers. And making a sizeable pile of glitter-coated money in the process.

I like to think that Elvie is immune to these girlie problems. Nothing makes her happier than covering her entire body in face paint, or actual paint, or mud. Or an indeterminate mixture of the three. She would happily spend her entire life naked if we let her. Which is either an indication of a very healthy self-image or a burgeoning career as a Miley Cyrus twerk-alike. I'm hoping for the former.

But here she is, despite all that paint and mud and nakedness. With this sudden awareness of 'beauty' and how it can be achieved. The feeling of not quite measuring up. At the age of three. Despite the fact that she is heart-stoppingly gorgeous, exactly as she is. And I'm stumped.

It's possible that I am partly responsible. I have a well-documented love affair with beautiful, impractical high heels, and Elvie has spent many wobbly hours trying to walk in my shoes. For several ill-advised months during her infancy I was an Avon lady. As a result of which she learnt to identify colours and body parts from eyeshadow charts and catalogue poses. Perhaps I should have seen this coming.

I've always worried about raising a girl. Because I was a girl. I know how hard it can be. I'm desperate for Elvie to find her voice. Her identity. The ability to be herself. I would so dearly love to see her grow up full of self-confidence. Immune to the media's nonsense. Thriving on who she is. On the inside. No sequins required.

I find it almost impossible to instil that level of confidence in myself. Let alone my daughter. I watch Elvie gravitate towards the popular girls at nursery and it ties my heart in knots. I want to protect her from the bitchiness, the caustic putdowns and the emotional bullying that took over my school-days. That still come back to bite me now. But I don't know how.

She is so beautiful. So unique. Such a quirk. I know that no matter how often I tell her, the voices of her peers will soon be louder and more influential than mine. I can't pick her friends. I can't control her thoughts. Most days I'm not even allowed to choose her clothes. This is just the beginning of the long, complicated journey of raising a girl.

There is, for the moment at least, one thing I can still control. The television. No more adverts. Not right now. We're sticking to CBeebies, until I figure out a plan.

When I do, we'll be unstoppable. With or without sequinned shoes.

Keeping up with Facebook.

This evening, Elvie and I made dinner. Meatballs. We're fancy like that. I think all the indoctrination-by-*Masterchef* is finally rubbing off. She wants to help. A lot.

I was tempted to announce our culinary adventure on Facebook. As you do. It would have gone something like this:

'Just made meatballs with my daughter. Amazing.'

Instantly there are images of matching aprons. Gingham, obviously. A tidy kitchen. Smiles and domestic bliss. Using the magic of Facebook to give my child-free friends a window into the idyllic world of parenting. And providing those who have spent the day dragging up their own children with yet another reason to feel like failures.

I resisted the smug status update. Because here's what actually happened:

Having begged me to let her help, Elvie tore herself away from her post-nursery cartoons, tried to roll one meatball, declared it to be too difficult, and spent the following five minutes bashing raw mince into the chopping board or wiping it over her dress. While Joel emptied an entire cupboard of food onto the floor. Elvie then refused to wash her hands because the water was 'too splashy.' Brief tantrum. Briefer hand washing. Eye rolling. At which point the lure of *Octonauts* won out and they both disappeared to the sofa, leaving me to tidy up. And finish cooking.

Both versions of this story are true. The status update and the kitchen carnage. But only the second one is real.

Let's be real. I dare you. You'll feel so much better for it. And so will everyone else.

Sleep training. In a nutshell.

Sleeping like a baby.

Ha.

I am of the firm belief that whoever coined that expression did not, in fact, have children of their own. (I wish I could take the credit for this observation. Sadly I can't. I saw it on a Nando's toilet wall. I know. You wish you were this classy.)

In reality, sleeping like a baby means sitting bolt upright and screaming as soon as your bedroom door is closed. Even though you were passed-out, stone-cold asleep twenty seconds ago. It means teasing your parents with three nights of unbroken sleep, only to completely lose the plot for the rest of the month. And, in our house, it means napping for no more than thirty minutes at a stretch, for fear that you might be missing out on the Best Time Ever. The reality of which is invariably a semi-comatose Mummy, flat out on the sofa, trying to finish a cup of tea while it's still warm.

Lack of sleep presents other challenges as well. Most noticeably, Wes crashing around, muttering about how he refuses to 'live in a silent house.' Whilst I curse him. Under my breath, obviously. Noble and idealistic as those words undoubtedly are, they don't stop the baby waking up when a saucepan falls off the draining board, or the front door is shut too loudly, or someone dares to attempt a conversation in the upstairs hallway.

I would venture to suggest that maybe, just maybe, those days are coming to an end. Nearly. We're definitely over the worst. Elvie has night terrors every couple of weeks, but as a general rule they're over by 9.30. Even I'm not in bed by then. Admittedly, last night I was up three times; Joel needing a cuddle, Elvie convinced that I'd forgotten her bedtime prayers and then an inexplicable 3 a.m. tantrum. Hers, not mine. This time. In spite of all of this, we're sneaking up on a place where we can go to bed and expect a good few hours of joined up sleep.

Unless of course Elvie 'loses her squeak up the chimney' as she did in the early hours of Thursday morning and absolutely has to 'go for a drive in the car to get it.' Seriously. I have no idea.

It feels good to finally be approaching a sustainable sleeping pattern. Three and a half years into parenting. To have some level of confidence in what we're doing. And how we've got there. To feel like we might just be getting something right.

Last night I made a mistake. One that I've made so many times, and always pretend I'll never make again.

It started so innocently. An article by a blogger I love, about how she'd managed to solve her daughter's sleep issues. Informative, fun, well balanced and, whilst obviously favouring her own particular style, not passing judgement on anyone else. So far, no problem.

But there was a link. I clicked it. Which led to more links. I clicked those too. Error. Twenty minutes later I was knee-deep in a band of militant American homeschoolers for whom any kind of bedtime routine constitutes an infringement of human rights.

Hey presto. Guilt. Confusion. Doubt. The worry that perhaps, after all, we've got everything wrong.

Nothing stirs up parental emotions so easily as sleep. There is nothing else that we're so fixated on. I read three pages of one bestselling book on the subject and felt like a failure before Elvie was even born. There was no way all those routines and timings and precise measurements were going to fit my personality, or my life. The book went straight back to the charity shop. And I was left to hunt out another guru.

Unfortunately, Elvie has never been a fan of sleeping. Not even as a baby. Unless it was daytime. Or she was feeding. Or being bounced up and down. By the time she was four months old, the only thing on my Christmas list was sleep. Preferably in blocks of more than an hour. I'd basically been napping for months.

I was beyond it. I woke up on Boxing Day at my parents' house, and cried for hours. Heaving, snotty, sobbing tears. I couldn't face going home. Having to cook, and clean, and look after a baby. I was just too tired. Too tired to move. We stayed a few extra days, and eventually made it back. By which time depression's filthy claws were well and truly in.

When she hit six months, Elvie still wouldn't sleep. We were desperate. I was depressed. Wes was exhausted. So we let her cry it out. For three nights. Which isn't the sort of thing you're supposed to admit to in public.

It worked wonders. She sleeps really well. Most of the time. Apart from the nightmares. And the missing teddy bears. And the crumpled duvets and the strange shadows and the nights when she loses her squeak. Obviously.

Joel has been different. And so have we. He's much more tactile. Much less independent. Much more likely to fall asleep in his highchair.

He's spent a lot more time in our bed. Even now, at thirteen months, he gets cuddled to sleep every night. And every nap time. We've slept a lot better. I think. Perhaps we've just been less stressed.

I've devoured sleep tactics over the last three years. Every parent does. Desperate for anything that might work. And it's just made me feel guilty. Attachment parenting advocates tell me that I've destroyed Elvie's trust and her ability to form emotional bonds. Hardcore disciplinarians tell me that I'm spoiling Joel. That he'll grow up to be a clingy, needy mummy's boy. That he'll never leave home.

Clearly these 'experts' have to hold strong positions. They won't sell any books otherwise. But scaring parents into following your sleep plan doesn't seem fair.

No two babies are the same. No two parents are the same. No two situations are the same. One baby can require wildly different tactics within the space of a week. As can their parents.

Sometimes I have the patience to rock my toddler indefinitely. Sometimes I desperately need to sleep, in order to be a better mummy during the daylight hours. Some nights my children need a bit more comfort. Some nights Mummy needs a bit more space.

I wrote a sleep training book today. It's short. It goes like this...

Do. Whatever. You. Need. To. Do.

That's it.

Sleep is important. Do what works for you. Be kind to yourself. And your baby. Do it deliberately. And do it with pride.

And please, no late-night link-clicking. That stuff can really keep you awake.

The 'B' word.

No, not that one. Or that one. Or even that one. Full marks for effort though. Now, drag your mind out of the gutter and we'll get started.

I got a letter this morning. Full commitment from the postal service in the raging midst of St Jude's storm, which has so far failed to shift the empty watering can that we foolishly left unattended in the garden.

It was from my therapist. The letter, not the watering can. Confirming the conversation that we had on Friday. My scores are down, I am officially into recovery and they are discharging me. Leaving me in the capable hands of my doctor, my pills and a few remaining computerised therapy sessions. I am, in their professional opinion, getting 'better'.

It's great news. Obviously. It's also terrifying.

I've got used to being ill. The numbness. The hiding. Avoiding difficult conversations and never putting myself out there. Hours of mindless television, curled up on the sofa. The constant exhaustion. The cloud of gloom on my shoulders.

It's been miserable. No doubt about that. But there's been a strange safety in it. In knowing where I stand, and what I can expect from my day. Even if that's absolutely nothing. When you're numb and exhausted, you don't get excited about anything. You don't invest in anything. You don't have anything to lose.

And now, here I am. On the verge of 'better'. Planning anniversary outings. Getting more than a little giddy as the first waves of Christmas arrive on the High Street. Exercising, for goodness sake. Enjoying my children. Occasionally. Really enjoying them, for the first time in months. Taking my tablet every morning and praying that I don't go backwards.

It feels like the first icy moments of a winter's morning.

Before the heating comes on. That thirty second gap between the warmth of the duvet and the pulling on of the jumper. Or the slippers. Or the dressing gown. Someone's pulled my blankets away and I'm not quite dressed yet. Everything's raw and fresh and uncomfortable. No wonder I hate mornings.

I still get hurt. I still get tired. I still get annoyed when Wes comes home from a week away with work and ventures to suggest that perhaps I could have hoovered in his absence. Hoovered? Seriously? I still get cross when I'm elbowed in the stomach by small children, or smacked round the head with a blunt object. There is no magic cure.

I know that all these conversations about emotions and feelings and hopes and plans are helpful. Important, even. But they're excruciatingly difficult. It would be so much easier to curl up under my blanket with some cake. I'm only now realising that yesterday's post-church sponge pudding purchase was motivated more by hoovergate than any legitimate physical need for sugar.

I'm trying to take my lead from Joel. He's almost fourteen months old. At that delicious stage where you can tell what he's trying to say, although the actual words are fuzzy. One that he's nailed is 'bye.' He's got that down. To the point where actually it's a little offensive. Like he just can't wait to get rid of you.

He's utterly unafraid of it. There's nothing scary about goodbye. Not to him. It's just a way of getting to the next activity. Meeting the next entertaining friend. He doesn't fret for hours or days or weeks about what he's leaving behind. He's straight on to something better. Better.

I'd like a bit of that. I'm up for looking forwards, rather than staring back at that desperate, constricting cosiness through some ludicrous rose-tinted window. Baby steps. That's all it takes. I hope. One step at a time. Forwards. Even though it's cold, and scary and uncomfortable.

Trusting that, in amongst the vulnerability and the risk and the rawness, 'better' will be exactly that. Better. Not perfect. Not fixed. Just better.

That'll do.

Gratitude and pumpkins-that-taste-of-nothing.

Let's get this over with. I'm not a fan of Halloween.

I love fancy dress. I love decorating my house. I love parties and sweets and traditions. I love the idea of something special to make these cold-and-dark-but-not-quite-Christmas days a little bit more bearable.

I'm not so keen on the witches. Or the devils. Or the ghosts or the skeletons. Or the groups of teenage vampires demanding sweets at my doorstep who would, on any other night of the year, find themselves reported to the police.

To be honest, I'm not even keen on the pumpkins. No wonder people carve them, because they're certainly not worth cooking. How anything so colourful can taste of so little is a mystery.

Sometimes it's good to poke fun at the things that scare us. I get that. But I've always been spectacularly bad at dealing with anything supernatural. Horror films, ghost stories, haunted houses. Not good. Even *Doctor Who*. Nightmares for weeks. Halloween is tricky for me – jokes or not. I suspect that Elvie is the same.

And yet, there's the fancy dress and the decorating. The parties and the sweets and the traditions. There has to be a way to have my tasteless-pumpkin-based-dessert and eat it.

I'm finding myself increasingly drawn to the American way of doing things. For possibly the first time ever. I'm no expert. My entire investigation has been conducted via the medium of Pinterest. But it appears that across the pond Halloween is a bit more generic. More a celebration of autumn and harvest and fun. Not so much with the demons. Please, America, correct me if I'm wrong.

Alongside my Halloween musings, I've been wondering about how to be a more spiritual parent. How to build wonder, awe and ritual into the lives of my tiny two. Inspired partly by the beautiful families that we do life with on a daily basis, and partly by the fact that depression has shrunk my own capacity for wonder and awe. And I really want it back.

All this thinking has given me a migraine. On the plus side, it's brought me back to Brené Brown. I may have mentioned her before. She is a big fan of gratitude. The power it has to transform your life. To give you back your energy and your perspective. It sounds amazing. But I'm spectacularly bad at it.

I excel at scarcity. My first thought in the morning is always, 'I need more sleep.' No matter how much I actually got. I deal in negatives and lack and 'not enough' from the moment I'm awake. Trust me, it stays with you. All day.

Apparently, the best weapon against scarcity is gratitude. Counting the hours I did sleep. Being grateful for two bouncing bundles of crazy to start my day with. And for my medication, to ensure that we all make it to bedtime in one piece.

It's not easy. It's a struggle. But I'd love my kids to grow into grateful people. Which means that I need to model gratitude. Urgh.

It needs to be fun. For my sake as well as theirs. There's no way I'll stick at it otherwise. And so, after much internet-trawling and craft-box raiding, here we are ... starting our own little Halloween tradition.

Allow me to introduce Project: Thankful Tree.

It's a tree. Or the outline of one, anyway. Made out of

paper. Blu-tacked on to the kitchen wall. And it's black. Turns out there's no brown paper in our art box. But I kind of love it. And so does Elvie.

I'm going to spend the next few days cutting leaves out of coloured paper. And then, every day for the month of November, we're going to think of something that we're thankful for, write it on a leaf and stick it to the tree. (Note to self: buy more blu-tack, hide the permanent markers.)

A new tradition. A ritual. A way to practice gratitude, as a family. And a celebration that we finally own our own house and no longer need to comply with landlords' 'no blu-tack' policies.

It doesn't solve the Halloween issue. But I've come to a solution that works. For now. Elvie and Joel are going to a party. A light party, at a local church. With a 'superhero' dress code. I'll have a bucket of sweets for the trick-or-treaters. And a huge sigh of relief that Wes will be home and I won't have to open the door myself.

Maybe next year we'll carve jack-o'-lanterns. Smiling ones. Put lights in them. We might even manage a Thanksgiving dinner. Provided I can find at least one half-decent pumpkin recipe.

For now, we'll be thinking of good things. Happy things. Thankful things. And hopefully we'll be nightmare-free. All of us.

I'd better get started on those leaves.

November

Why I'm using my pretty straws.

A few months ago, I was given some paper straws. Red and white and stripy. The ones that appear at every inconceivably beautiful children's party I've ever seen on Pinterest. I love them. Maybe a little too much. So much that I've never actually used them. I'm saving them for 'the right occasion'. Which may or may not exist.

Two years ago, I made chutney. Loads of it. Three different flavours. To give away as Christmas presents in a sadistic, entirely self-inflicted attempt to prove my status as a domestic goddess. I had a retro jar labelling set that Mum had given me after my brief foray into jam-making. Perfect. Did I use it? Of course not. I'm saving it for 'a special day.' So I made my own jar covers. Out of old t-shirts.

They were cute. And very thrifty. They were also entirely unnecessary and very time consuming. The pretty labels are still gathering dust in my kitchen cupboard, right next to the paper straws. Waiting for their big moment. Who knows how long they'll have to wait.

It's fair to say that I'm bad at living in the moment. In my defence, I excel at living in a fictional, unspecified middle-distance moment when everything will be perfect. It's the normal days that I struggle to appreciate. These days. The playgroup-lunch-nursery-dinner-bedtime-laundry-nappies-dishes days. I'm easily bored and frequently distracted. Which is not the best recipe for contentment.

Occasionally there are times when I'm shaken out of my

dissatisfaction. When my daydreaming and my moaning and my 'if only's' get knocked sideways. This week has been a prime example.

On Sunday we drove to London to meet our brand new nephew. Not even twelve hours old, utterly scrumptious and very heavy indeed.

At the same time, my parents were driving to Southampton, to say goodbye to their favourite uncle. Because his cancer was back, and aggressive, and he only had two weeks to live.

I can't quite comprehend it. On Thursday, while the children and I were bobbing for apples in a saucepan in the kitchen, my great-uncle and great-aunt got the news that would change their lives forever.

Two weeks.

He's too young. That's for sure. Barely older than my parents. Dying not as a result of vice, indulgence and a flagrant disregard for public health warnings, but because of the asbestos that he worked with for years, in order to feed his family.

There have been a lot of tears this week. A lot of angry prayers. God's suffered a fair share of name-calling. In my house at least.

It's. Just. Not. Fair.

He's a great man. You're supposed to say that when someone's dying. Everyone does. But this time it's true.

He's the one who took my mum to the funfair as a teenager, missed her curfew and got himself into a whole heap of trouble. He's the one she trusted to be godfather to her precious, poorly baby.

I was a bridesmaid for his daughter. Before his son recorded *Match of the Day* over the wedding video. Awkward.

He gave me my first sorbet. In his garden, on the grounds of the school where he worked. Lemon sorbet, from a huge chest freezer. It was twenty years ago, at least, but I still remember the fizz on my tongue. And how grown-up it made me feel. I've loved it ever since.

And his smile. The kind of smile that brings an entire room to life. If he's smiling at you, you feel like the centre of the universe. I'm pretty sure that everyone who meets him falls a little bit in love.

And yet, in a few days' time, he'll be gone. Forever. He's ready. Just about. We're not.

We saw him last Christmas. Celebrating the fact that he'd been given the all-clear. Pulling crackers and eating chocolates and wearing silly hats. Less than a year ago. It doesn't seem real.

I've often wondered what I'd do if I was told I had two weeks to live. I could write a list. Several lists. Each of them a mile long. It never occurred to me that, by the time I was given that timeframe, I'd be too sick to do anything other than say goodbye.

This week has been cruel. But it's taught me. There are no warnings. There is no time for lists. There is no indeterminately-far-off-perfect moment. It's these days that are the precious ones. The messy ones. The boring ones. The normal ones. These days. They're the only ones we've got.

We used the stripy paper straws at dinner time tonight. It wasn't 'a special occasion'. Not by a long way. We ate tuna pasta and talked about nursery. Elvie was so excited by the straw that she knocked her juice all over the table. It wasn't perfect. But all four of us were together. And healthy.

Right now, that counts for a lot.

Code brown.

Disclaimer Don't read this if you're squeamish. Or eating.

I'm aware that sometimes I can sound a little serious.

Worthy even. That occasionally, there's the faintest scent of someone who's getting her life together. Albeit very slowly. In the interest of fairness and honesty, here's a snapshot from today.

From my Elvie. Who spent this morning bobbing for apples. With her hands. That's my girl.

Potty training Elvie was a task. We started too early, after she began removing her own nappies and doing her business on the carpet in protest at the arrival of her baby brother.

By the time she was three, many months later, we had it down and apart from the initial fear of the nursery toilets, everything has gone smoothly ever since. So to speak.

Until this week. We've had something of a major regression. I have absolutely no idea why. But the evidence is inescapable. Wet tights. Little puddles. Piles of washing. But we've been spared the worst. Until now.

This morning I was smiling, telling a friend how Elvie cleaned herself up after our only recent 'code brown' incident. When I got upstairs to deal with it, there was nothing to be found. Turns out she'd flushed the evidence down the toilet. Knickers and all.

Oh, how we laughed.

This afternoon Elvie went upstairs for a wee. And didn't come down. For ages. She assured me that she was 'Fine, Mummy.' Fool that I am, I believed her.

Ten minutes later she finally reappeared. Without her tights. Or her knickers. Instead, she was wearing a pair of yellow shorts. Underneath her dress. In November.

Alarm bells.

'Elvie, where are your tights?'

'I took them off.'

'Why?'

'So they didn't go in the poo.'

Ah.

Thirty minutes, it took me. To clean the floor. And the toys. And her Dalmatian pyjamas. Which she'd used to wipe the carpet. Nice.

It was everywhere. Literally. Even along the bottom of the doorframe. I don't remember much of my GCSE physics but I'm pretty sure that shouldn't even be possible.

And the piéce de resistance? A huge pile in the middle of the floor. Topped with a toy spaceman. No really. She'd pushed him right in. As though he'd just conquered some steaming brown planet. It's impossible to turn off her quirk.

It was revolting. There are no other words. No polite ones, anyway.

Of course, given my wisdom, patience and excellent attitude to unexpected trauma, I cleaned up, came downstairs, smiled at my beautiful babies and got on with making dinner.

Like hell did I. In the real world, I spent ten minutes frantically scrubbing the smell from my hands before coming downstairs, refereeing an argument over the toy stethoscope, collapsing in front of CBeebies, and texting Wes to grab a takeaway on his drive home. Nailed it.

Last week I was wondering whether we were ready to ditch the night-time nappy pants. After today, I think we'll wait a while. If only for the sake of the spacemen.

Things I (haven't) learnt from nursery.

Elvie has been a 'nursery girl' for three months now. She loves it. So do we. It's just that we know nothing about it. Nothing at all. Not for want of trying.

Occasionally she comes home with irrefutable evidence of fun. Henna tattooed hands, or a firework picture. A Pudsey bear mask that's twice the size of her head. Sometimes I'll hear her singing songs that I've never heard before. Days of the week, or plodding donkeys, or how many hammers Peter required for his post-apocalyptic carpentry sessions.

Every so often she lets slip that she's learnt something. Like the time that Guy Fawkes managed to blow up the Houses of Parliament. Interesting. Last week I had to guess what she was creating from her orange peel. Apparently it was Ravana, the ten-headed god who killed Rama at Diwali. Looked like an octopus to me ....

These glimpses of her nursery life are rare. Mostly you could be forgiven for believing that she spends three hours a day in a cupboard. By herself.

I ask her about it. All the time. After she's recovered from the why-didn't-you-bring-my-scooter-I-need-it-every-day meltdown and is safely encamped on the sofa with juice and emergency raisins.

'How was nursery?'

There are three possible responses: 'Fine', 'Okay' or 'I'll tell you tomorrow'. I think we all know that tomorrow never comes.

Any information that I do manage to extract from her falls into one of three categories.

1) Illness/Injury

This is a particular favourite. Of Elvie's. Not mine.

'How was nursery?'

'Fine. Joshua had a high temperature and had to go home, and Eli had a bleed on his arm where he scratched it. And Maryam was sick on the carpet.'

Lovely. Mind you, the nursery plays its part in the great illness obsession. At least once a week we get a letter informing us of the head lice/chicken pox/ringworm that are plaguing the school. We even have a 'wet comb bug busting nit removal method' sheet stuck to our fridge. If that doesn't encourage weight loss I don't know what will.

The good news is, she's definitely not squeamish. The bad news is I've had to persuade her that head lice don't make great pets. And I'm not sure she's convinced.

2) Discipline
'How was nursery?'

'Fine. Max went on the red face because he hit the teacher and Kyle was on the amber face cos he didn't listen to what he was told, and I was on the green face and the diamond. All day.'

Usually followed by a sigh and some wistful middle-distance staring. Making it onto the red face is one of her greatest ambitions. Especially after the time she may or may not have been on the amber face after opening a box that she'd been told to leave alone. She informed us all, gleefully, as soon as she got home. And was distraught the following day when none of the teachers knew what she was talking about.

Perhaps it was a dream. Like the time I lost her in the park with the green gates while she was looking for a lollipop. She tells everyone about that as well.

3) Food
'How was nursery?'

'Fine. We had pears and carrots for snack time.'

Food is our most reliable source of nursery-based information. She's always happy to talk about food. Especially when her keyworker offers her snowmen's noses (carrots), Gruffalos' eyes (oranges) and sharks' fins (bananas. I know. Tenuous).

There's nothing better than snack time, as far as Elvie's concerned. Except perhaps an excruciating twelve-minute role play at dinner time where she re-enacts her job as drinks monitor and I am forced to make the agonising decision between milk and water. On behalf of every child in her class.

Even the food stories aren't foolproof. One day she announced that they had eaten crisps at snack time. Which seemed slightly at odds with the school's healthy eating policy. Turns out they were poppadums. For Eid. Last week she reliably informed me that they had eaten 'something sweet and orange and beginning with E'. Nope. Still not a clue.

I'm taking this lack of information as a positive thing. Choosing to believe that she's so settled that only an illness or a discipline infringement is worthy of comment. It's come as something of a surprise. I've been by her side constantly for the last three years, so it's strange to have whole hours in the day when I have no idea what she's up to. Strange. And wonderful.

Besides, I have my ways. There's a computer in the entrance hall, playing a slideshow of photographs at collection time. So I can see her beaming with delight from halfway up a tree, or her screwed up concentrating face as she learns to use the computer. I can see her sprawled out on the floor drawing enormous pictures with her friends. It would seem that she hasn't been shut in a cupboard after all.

Later this week there's a stay and play session. Where Joel and I are allowed in for the whole afternoon. Where I can see all the throwing up and not listening for myself. Maybe even get to eat some Gruffalos' eyes.

I can't wait.

Curling up at the edges. Or, why it's important to marry the right man.

Wes and I are closing in on our fifth wedding anniversary. Five whole years. Nothing short of a miracle.

It certainly hasn't gone according to plan.

I blame Disney. And every romantic comedy ever made.

All those stories of near-disaster, misunderstandings, evil stepmothers and talking woodland creatures have one thing in common. As soon as the wedding bells are over, so is the story.

They all live happily ever after. Don't ask questions.

That's what I was brought up on. I devoured it. And, despite my best efforts to find books about twins who love recycling, or little girls who play with tigers, Elvie devours it too. There's nothing she loves more than a princess. Except perhaps a princess who lives in a cake.

She plays weddings a lot. Talks about the dresses. The flowers. The dancing. In her mind, it's the first dance that seals the deal. She's going to be a menace at school discos.

The wedding is the goal. The big day. The big dress. The princess moment.

To be married. To be chosen. Publicly. And loved forever.

Nothing wrong with that.

I'll be the first to admit that, even as a stony-hearted twentysomething, I desperately wanted someone to pick me. To love me.

And then he did.

He walked into my life one night at a networking event, and went home with my phone number and a spring in his step. I hadn't even realised he was hitting on me and, slightly embarrassingly, I couldn't remember his name. It was Wes.

He'd said he'd call me. And he actually did. We went out for a lunch date that lasted eight hours, discovered we had half the world in common, and quickly became inseparable. I was swept off my feet. I'd never imagined that anybody could love me so well. So completely. Warts and all.

Things got serious very quickly. I moved to be with him. Leaving behind my London, my life, and the best friends I'd ever known.

That's when it got messy. I had a deep-rooted fear

of abandonment. He had previous-girlfriend-induced commitment issues. It wasn't pretty.

We broke up a few times. I cried. A lot. But we never managed to stay apart.

And then, in the midst of yet another standoff, at the point where I had deleted his number from my phone so that I couldn't send him any more ridiculously over-emotional texts, he snuck into my garden in the middle of the night to propose via the medium of tealights.

There were flowers. There was a ring. Quite possibly sub-zero temperatures. It was beautiful. I was taken completely by surprise, and so stunned that I spent the rest of the night talking about garden gnomes and woke up wondering if I'd dreamt the whole thing.

If this was a Disney film, or a Richard Curtis comedy, it would all end there. With a few token shots of the wedding to fill the closing credits.

It wasn't a movie. Thank goodness. That was just the beginning.

We had a fairly disastrous honeymoon. It's much more common than you think. It turns out that France in December is really cold. Especially when you have a throat infection. And exhaustion. And barely any hot water. Thank goodness for Disneyland Paris. It's hard to be grumpy there.

Mickey Mouse was good respite. I spent most of our first year of marriage wondering why more people don't get divorced. I suspect Wes did too. I went on the pill, and felt as though I had lost my mind. I learnt the hard way that I'm more selfish than I'd ever imagined. That I don't appreciate having to compromise. I sulked. I snarled. I was passive-aggressive. And eventually Wes started to run out of patience.

We booked a long holiday. To celebrate making it to our first anniversary. South Africa and India. A month away. It was incredible. Sun, adventure and cocktails. Just what we needed. By the time we came back I was pregnant. The next four years were a blur of pregnancy, small babies, toddlers and post-natal depression. Which brings us to now.

There have been days when we've shouted. Or not spoken at all. Endless snaps, and losses of temper. He's realised that I don't notice when a room needs hoovering. I've discovered that he has an unbreakable resistance to washing up. I've figured out that it's best to feed him before attempting a serious conversation. He's learnt not to expect a constructive response to anything before 7.30 a.m.

There have been days, sometimes weeks on end, when I've wondered if he liked me at all. There have been days when I certainly didn't like him. Days when we've argued for hours over nothing at all. Or given in too quickly on the important things. Days when I knew he was going to leave me. Days when I would have left me. Plenty of those.

And yet, nearly five years on, we're still here. Still married. Still celebrating. By the skin of our teeth.

These last few years have been a learning curve. A steep one. With a few entirely unnecessary tests thrown in for fun. I'm not sure what grade we'd get. But we'd pass. I know that much.

Not by chance. Or luck. Or magic. Through gritted teeth and determination. Because of those gut-wrenchingly vulnerable moments in the clear air of the morning when we've turned around and apologised. As a result of those tiny little tiptoe steps back towards romance in the wake of our most bitter arguments.

All of those raw, painful, wearing-our-hearts-on-the-outside moments have got us to today. To a place where we are starting to appreciate each other again. Really, properly appreciate each other. It's been a long time coming.

Recently I had a blip in my recovery process. The endless crusade against Churchill's big black dog. Maybe because I'm tired or because I've been trying to do too much too soon. Maybe the wind has changed. Who knows.

By the time I went to bed on Friday I was starting to fold in on myself. All I wanted to do, for the entire weekend, was hide.

Wes was amazing. He asked me how I was. I told him I was curling up at the edges. And he understood. Completely. I couldn't face the firework display on Saturday night. So he took the children. And I stayed on the sofa with a blanket.

Yesterday, he left me in bed when the children got up. When I surfaced, they were tidying the living room shelves, which have been a jumble of piled-high clutter since we moved in. Months ago. Because he knew.

He knew that physical chaos makes my mental chaos worse. He knew that I wouldn't have the motivation to tidy. He knew that it would lift my mood. And it did.

He's the only one who knows me, faults, flaws, hoover-resistance and all. Inside out. And still loves me. He still kisses me, even after two huge babies turned my stomach into what can only be described as a saggy map of the London Underground.

He knows which mug to put my 'I-need-some-comfort' tea in. He knows when I need his arm around me to hold me up. He knows how to stand his ground in a French theme-park queue. And how to give me hope.

Five years in. It hasn't been plain sailing. It's bloody hard work.

But it's worth it. Absolutely.

Happily ever after would be nice. But I'd rather have this. I'd rather have Wes.

Prince Charming may be perfect, but I bet he's dull. And he doesn't tidy shelves.

When God brings a blanket.

A friend once told me that depression is a bitch. On balance, I have to agree.

I've never experienced anything else that makes you feel so alone. Isolated. Unworthy.

Since I've been writing, people have asked me where God is in all this mess. Which has made me stop. Pause. And consider. Finally, I have an answer.

I'll be honest.

First time around, I didn't find Him at all. It was a big dark hole and it was all my very own. Mostly because I kept it to myself. Only two people outside of my immediate family even knew that I was depressed.

I kept it to myself, and I fixed it by myself. I went to therapy and I did my homework. Most of the time. I took on all the information I was given and by the time Elvie turned one I could breathe again.

Well done me.

I certainly didn't see God in it.

This time everything is different. Thanks to a ridiculous moment of truth-telling before the whole congregation, everyone at church knows. Thanks to their amazing reaction and relentless encouragement, I started writing. And now the world knows.

This is definitely the way forward.

I can't count the number of people who've come alongside me. Called, texted, hugged. Given me chocolate. Supported Wes. Looked after the children. And loved me. Really, truly loved me. Even when I was in pieces. In a way that I would never have let them before.

I've seen God there. In the faithfulness and the care. In the emails and the phonecalls and the notes. From the ones who know Him, and the ones who don't.

That has been amazing. Humbling. But there's more.

I'm learning a lot about myself. And God. And how we work. Most of it is brand new.

Friends have seen me edging my way towards recovery,

read the blog, got excited by all the potential and said, 'Now you know why He let this happen.'

I can't agree. Not my God. That's not the way He works.

There are genetic factors. Stress. Exhaustion. My body's utter inability to deal with extra hormones. Plenty of reasons. None of which involve some great cosmic character test.

He didn't put me in this position. I suspect that the whole sorry saga is breaking God's heart as much as it's breaking ours. But He's moving. And He's working. In amongst it all. And He's dragging something precious out of all this dirt.

It's the start of a new relationship. Shy, tentative, awkward. Like all the great love affairs. It's come as a real surprise.

I was brought up to believe that what you *do* is important. That if you work hard, good things happen. That you do your bit. I spent my teenage years in an all-girls grammar school that valued achievement above all else, leaving precious little space for creativity. It wasn't the kind of environment where you learnt from your mistakes. You shouldn't have made them in the first place.

Subconsciously, that's how I've always related to God. Pointing out what I can do for Him. How lucky He is to have me on the team. It's been a bit of a blow to realise that I've been in church for my entire life and known all the answers. But I've never known Him. Not really.

This time round, depression has brought me lower than low. And I've been a terrible Christian. Swearing instead of praying. Reading John Lewis catalogues rather than the Bible. Going to church purely so that I could use the crèche facilities and get half-an-hour's break from my children.

I've been a bad wife and an uncaring mother. I've been selfish and insular and aggressive.

I couldn't fix myself. Not this time. Therapy wasn't enough. I've ended up taking the very medication that I've always looked down on so freely.

I couldn't even pretend to be any use to anyone. Not my family. Not my friends. Certainly not God.

And yet.

He loved me.

At my lowest and my worst.

He surrounded me with friends to hold my hand. He held my babies. He held me.

He gave Wes the strength to stand by my side. Gave me the strength to go to the doctors. To take the tablets.

He gave me everything I needed. When I had nothing to offer in return.

Where was God in it all? Right here.

He wasn't looking down from on high; waiting for me to pull myself together, chipper up and be useful again. He was with me. Down here. In the hole. Bringing blankets. And a little tiny torch. Because a glimpse of light was all that I could handle.

I've been in church for thirty years. I've heard a lot about grace. And I never ever understood it. Until now.

I'm not 'fixed' yet. Not even close. But that doesn't matter. I know now. I get it.

God loves me. Me. Actual me.

Not who I *could* be. Not the best possible version of me. Not the perfect Pinterest mother. Me.

The woman who cuts a hole in her own dress twenty seconds after giving her daughter the 'safety with scissors' talk.

The woman whose son wears wellies, even when the sun shines, because she can't find his other shoes.

The woman who eventually changes her children's bedsheets after finding patches of mould on the old ones.

I'm messy, a little bit sweary, and still not sure if I could find my Bible.

But God loves me. Just as I am.

I will be grateful.

Forever.

WINTER

December

Turning 31. Eventually.

This time last year I turned thirty. Which felt like a pivotal moment, as do most birthdays that end in zero. I was planning the celebrations. We were buying a house. By the time my birthday arrived, we'd have moved in. Settled. Unpacked. And I'd have a party. A birthday/ housewarming party. With the emphasis on housewarming. That way I wouldn't have to be fabulous all night. If it all got too much and I sloped off for a meltdown, everyone could admire the carpets. Or the curtains. Or the walls. Either way, there would definitely be a party. Preferably with fancy dress. After all, you're only thirty once.

The house fell through. We were well and truly gazumped. When my birthday finally arrived, we were knee-deep in negotiations on another. Complete with a toddler and a two-month-old baby.

There was no party.

Instead my parents watched the children for a few hours so that Wes and I could eat steak and chips at our local pub. By ourselves. With no interruptions. Other than the landlady, the barman and a drag queen clambering over our table to hang Christmas lights. Of course. They even bought me a Mars Bar with a candle in. Accompanied by a rousing chorus of 'Happy Birthday dear Sarah.' Which would have been nicer if that *was* my name.

This year I decided that I would turn thirty again. Do it properly. Redeem the slightly disappointing events of last

December. Do something sparkly. Something fun.

I didn't. I turned thirty-one. Because of a little black box that arrived completely unexpectedly. Tied with purple and white ribbon. Lined with velvet. Two teardrop pearl earrings nestled snugly inside. Beautiful. Gleaming. And a total surprise.

My thirty-first birthday present from Wes. Pearls. Real pearls. Proper I'm-a-grown-up-now jewellery. He chose them because they were pretty. A little bit unusual. Not your average pearl studs. I fell in love with them instantly. Because they are perfect.

Tear drops. Beautiful tear drops.

It's taken me years to get used to the idea of crying. Vulnerability. Emotions in general. My default setting has always been humour. Deflection. The more observant ones among you may have noticed that already. Throughout my teens and twenties I took a quiet pride in the fact that I was hard as nails. Infamous amongst my friends for never shedding a tear, regardless of what happened. I said 'hardcore', they said 'heart of stone'. In jest. Mostly.

In reality, I'm not built like that. Underneath it all I'm actually very sensitive. I need a good cry every so often. Very often. Who knew? Wes has always been an advocate of my emotional awakening – determined to dig beneath the surface. Wanting to understand the 'real me'. Despite the fact that even I don't know exactly what that entails. There's a reason so many people tell him that he's brave.

Slowly, slowly, my emotions are gaining back some ground. Depression hasn't helped, but the hormones of pregnancy and motherhood certainly have. In the last couple of years I've cried at *The X Factor* finals, home improvement shows, department store Christmas adverts and, more importantly, real life events. Tears come much more easily now – whether of sadness or joy. I prefer the joy.

I get it. I honestly do. It's better to feel things, I know.

But I'm still coming round to the idea that tears can be beautiful. Healing. Sacred. I'm a pretty good student, but I learn lessons like this about twelve times a week. And forget them again instantly. Unless.

Unless I have something physical. To hold on to. Something that acts as a reminder, every time I look at it. Something to nudge me on my stubborn days. Something that whispers truth when I'm not listening. Which is most days.

These earrings are just that. A physical reminder, hanging from my earlobes.

This has been a year of grit and dirt and imperfection. But occasionally, just occasionally, grit gets turned to pearls. It's been a year of tears. Heavy, snotty, messy tears. But sometimes, just sometimes, tears are precious. It's been a year. Not a fun one or a sparkly one, or a perfect one. I'll leave that to the jewellery.

But it has been a year. It counts. I can't just wish it away. I'm not sure I want to.

I'm thirty-one. And you know what, that might just be okay.

Living at John Lewis.

I love Christmas. Really love it. There are very few first-world problems that can't be eased by an hour in the John Lewis Christmas department. All those decorations, hung up so beautifully. All the gifts so neatly arranged. All the fairy lights sparkling. Not a single bulb blown. Meandering my way through a perfect vision of a snow-capped festive idyll. It's like therapy. But cheaper. Unless you buy anything, of course.

I've always loved this time of year. The magic, the excitement, the glitter. It's been my absolute favourite since I was a very small girl. These days, it's a touch more stressful.

Because I'm the one in charge. It's my job to make the magic happen. Which is hard work. Especially when you're a perfectionist.

Since becoming a Mum, I've spent every December in a state of abject panic. Worrying that Elvie will be the only child at nursery without an 'elf on the shelf'. Panicking about when I'll get time to make the homemade jam that is obviously an intrinsic part of every gift. Fretting about whether I've spent too much money. Or too little. Distraught that I haven't decorated my house as beautifully as those wretched Internet Women. Knowing beyond a doubt that I will fail to provide the spectacular festive experience that my children obviously deserve.

It's exhausting. No wonder so many mothers spend Christmas afternoon curled up in a heap on the sofa. I'm not sure I'll make it that far.

Last Christmas was subdued, to say the least. We'd moved house ten days earlier, with a potty training toddler and a three month old. Which is more than enough to screw up anyone's plans. There were no clove-scented candles or cutesy Scandinavian-themed decorations. Mostly just cardboard boxes. And paracetamol. We survived. We even had a little bit of fun. But the magic was missing. For me, at least. Not even the mulled wine could hide it.

It's fair to say that this year, I've attacked Christmas with a vengeance. In an unprecedented feat of organisation, almost all the shopping is done. Which only leaves the wrapping, baking, making and writing. Or, as I like to call it, 'the fun part'. This time, I'm aiming at perfect.

This morning we went shopping. Me and the littlies, for some last-minute items before the traditional extended-family gathering this weekend. It was a bad idea from the start. Elvie was shattered. So was Joel. So was I. But we needed mini-marshmallows, and gift bags, and ribbon. So we went.

We were late leaving, late getting home and late making

lunch. Which is more critical than it sounds. Nursery starts at 12:30 and apparently it's bad form to drop them off unfed. I was flustered, and rushed. The children were exhausted. There was shouting. There were tears. There was bread and cheese for lunch. And absolutely no cake.

We made it to nursery on time. Just. I dropped her off, smiling, doing my best impression of a perfectly-normal-mummy-who-is-not-actually-shaking-with-rage-on-the-inside. I think I got away with it. I hope. Then I came home, put Joel down for his nap and tried to drag myself out of the whirlpool of guilt that currently takes up the space where my brain used to be. Yes, she'd been whinging. And back chatting. All day. But I'm the grown-up here. At least, I think I am.

Perhaps I'm not quite as close to better as I thought. Perhaps I should take things a bit easier. Perhaps not every present needs to be quirkily gift-wrapped. Or handmade. Perhaps perfect is way out of reach.

My favourite game at the moment is 'at least'. At least I didn't say anything I regret. At least she's curled up by my side now watching telly, all tears forgotten. At least this happened now, on December 3rd. With twenty-two days left until Christmas.

There's still time to apologise. Time to make amends. Time to search for that elusive Christmas spirit.

I'm pretty sure they sell it at John Lewis.

Real life lullabies.

You know that moment, when you find something that is hilarious and brave and full of truth, and then you share it with someone else and they look at you like perhaps you've lost your mind? Yes? That. I've had that this week.

All because of Tim Minchin. I'm a massive fan. Let's

get that on the record straight away. I love what he does with words. How surprising he makes them. The way he's always one step ahead. He's probably my all-time favourite Australian. Sorry Kylie.

Last week Wes and I finally made it to see *Matilda* in the West End. If you get the chance, see it. Please. It's outrageously good. The choreography, the set, the acting. And the lyrics. Especially the lyrics. We laughed out loud. Several times. We cried. We were first on our feet for what is surely the obligatory standing ovation. So when a friend played me another Minchin masterpiece, I was certain that Wes would share the love. Not so much, apparently.

The song in question is 'Lullaby'.

Disclaimer Before you play it, make sure any children are out of earshot. Or wear headphones. Don't listen to it if you struggle with: a) strong language; b) brutal honesty, or c) both.

Parental guidance over, feel free to YouTube it. Whilst you ponder when exactly YouTube became a verb.

Done? Great.

Let's talk.

I must have listened to this song a hundred times this week, and every time it provokes an actual physical reaction inside of me. The lyrics, those frenzied violins, the nervous laughter of the audience. His 'seriously people, I'm telling the truth' face.

When I played it to Wes, and to Elvie's godfather, they both had the same reaction. Intake of breath, pursing of lips and the pronouncement that it had, in their opinion, crossed 'some sort of line'.

Not so much for me. For me, the song is a kick in the guts. It's as though someone had seen inside the furthest reaches of my brain at the darkest points of the longest nights when exhaustion was at its peak and it was 4 a.m. and the morning was coming and the baby still wouldn't sleep. A kick in the guts, followed by a huge exhale. Because finally I had an acknowledgement that, no matter how awful things get inside my head in the tiniest little hours, I am not the only one. Somebody understands.

I'm beginning to realise just how important that is.

How important it is to admit that, away from the magazines and the status updates and the Pinterest boards, parenting is tough. Really, really tough. Sometimes you're winning, and other times you're crushed into the ground. And it's so easy to feel as though you're alone.

I remember lying awake through the night. Envying the parents with babies in special care, because at least they could sleep for more than an hour at a time. Sometimes, fleetingly, I would envision a need for hospitalisation – for me or for the baby. And smile.

I remember walking the buggy down the road and contemplating briefly, fleetingly, what it would feel like to push it in front of a bus. Walking downstairs, baby in arms, and pondering what would happen if I 'fell'. Wondering how long it would take to reunite us if I just left the baby somewhere. How much sleep I could get in the meantime.

Sleep deprivation is truly hideous. So is depression. But worst of all is the way they make you feel. As though actually, it's you that's hideous. Horrible. Shameful. Unfit to be a mother. As though nobody else understands. And if you tried to tell them they'd breathe in, purse their lips and tell you that you'd crossed 'some sort of line'.

Perhaps some parents never have these thoughts. I envy them. Hugely. But I'm willing to bet that most mothers, most fathers, do. At least a little. I know, from personal experience, that it's not in the top three Toddler-Group-Conversation-

Starters. 'So, you know those moments when you feel utterly wretched and have terrible thoughts and believe in your heart of hearts that you're an awful mother? I have them too – turns out you're normal. Fancy a custard cream?'

It's not an easy subject to broach. But it's desperately important. To find people who understand. Who can share the darkest, hardest points of parenthood. Not just the first steps and the graduations and the swimming badges. Without that support, it's all in our heads. Going round and round. Getting bigger and bigger. Trust me, that's bad news. I should know.

It's a tough conversation to start. I know that too. But find the right people to have it with and you might just feel like a whole new person. Or less of a monster, at least. Still winning.

In the meantime, I promise you this:

One day, your children will sleep.

And so will you.

Things will get better. Maybe with medication. Maybe with therapy. Maybe with time, and tea, and lots of tissues. But it will get better.

And so will you.

You. Are. Not. The. Only. One.

At the very least there's me, my friend and Tim Minchin. That's got to be worth a custard cream.

Christmas stops here. Kind of.

I've been trying. I really have. Trying to let go of my misty-eyed dream of that elusive perfect Christmas. The one that's full of mini marshmallows and gingerbread houses and homemade jam. It turns out that it's not the fight for perfect that's been driving me mad. It's just being. In general. And doing. Christmas in particular.

It's been a stressful week. Finding babysitters. And

nativity costumes. Making doctors' appointments. And attending them. Keeping the children occupied at my wonderful Great-Uncle's funeral. Making the family's presents. Wrapping the family's presents. Remembering nursery Christmas jumper day. Buying the Christmas jumper. Forgetting what to take to toddler group parties. And where I've hidden the Christmas cards.

That's just for starters. That's without my head nagging me that I've missed all the overseas posting dates, that my children haven't had a bath for days, and that it's not normal to spend twenty minutes every morning searching through a mountain of clean washing for socks. Any socks. Even if they don't match.

Most of this week I haven't known what day it is. To be honest, I haven't known much. Except that I can't go on like this for long without having some kind of nervous breakdown. 'Not having a nervous breakdown' is pretty high on my Christmas list this year. In fact, it's right at the top.

This morning we were at a toddler group Christmas party. There was food and a puppet show. Santa came round with presents. Joel freaked out. Everyone ate way more sugar than they should at that time of day. The usual.

As we were leaving, one of the dear sweet helpers who gives up every Wednesday morning to serve us tea and keep us sane, asked me whether I was ready for Christmas.

It's a simple question. Standard December small-talk. I gave her a standard December small-talk answer.

'Oh, not really. But it will happen anyway, won't it. It always does...'

Halfway home I stopped. In amidst the scootering and the mushroom-buying and the nursery drop-off. I stopped. And I thought.

What if it was true?

That I don't have everything ready, but Christmas will happen anyway. And it will be great.

I couldn't stop thinking about it.

What if I just stopped preparing? Stopped stressing? Drew a line in the sand and said 'I'm done. Time to have some fun.'

What if I stopped caring so much about the unmade paper chains and the lists of handmade 'little extra' gifts I was planning? What if I decided that we had enough decorations up already? That my cupboard was so full of presents waiting to be wrapped that I just wasn't going to buy any more?

Elvie won't care if the napkins aren't folded into origami swans. Joel won't mind if the chutney comes from Tesco. I'm pretty sure Wes would rather have me in one piece than a homemade woodland-themed table decoration.

It's a bold new plan. But I like it. I feel three stone lighter already.

The timing is perfect. Tomorrow we'll be halfway through Advent. Twelve out of twenty-four. Twelve days for planning and preparing and Internet shopping. And then ... stop. No ifs, no buts. If it's not done by the end of the twelfth, it's not done.

There are presents that still need wrapping. But now I can do that in the evenings, with a mug of mulled apple juice and a Christmas movie. Without stressing that I should be hanging holly from the staircase or making four different kinds of fudge.

There are family visits to be made. Church services to attend. Christmas parties to be had. But now I can be there in mind as well as in body. Now I can enjoy them. Without begrudging the time that I could have spent writing gift labels or last minute shopping.

I may well make mince pies. Or paint something Christmassy. But my hope is that now, that can be a laid-back family activity. Without counting the minutes until we need to move on to the next tightly-scheduled 'really-fun-thing'.

I am reliably informed that Advent is, in fact, about quieting ourselves. About thinking and hoping and dreaming. Waiting and being still. Being. Just being.

There hasn't been much of that around here lately.

Probably because it's scary. Daring to believe that I'm more than just the sum of what I achieve. That I don't have to provide the biggest, best, most original pile of presents in order to be loved. That my family would rather I snuggled up with them under a blanket watching festive telly than lost my mind cooking up a gourmet feast in the kitchen.

That Christmas will be okay. Just as it is.

Because I am okay. Just as I am.

Even if I can't find any socks.

After the Christingle.

The flame is out.
Ribbon unravelled.
Pins and cocktail sticks abandoned.
The fruits of the four corners of the earth have been devoured by the little girl with the marshmallow breath.

All that remains is the scent.
Orange. Frankincense.
Staining my fingers.
Seeping into my soul.

A pause. A beat. A flicker.

And so, to tomorrow.
With joy.

And a song that sounds like love.

January

Gently does it.

I'm good at New Year's Resolutions. Making them, anyway. Most years I have a list. Not too short, not too long. Nothing wildly overambitious, but still an inherent element of challenge. And preferably at least one task that I've almost completed. It's good to get something crossed off early.

It's an art form. One that I am well on my way to perfecting. Writing the list can take an entire day. Decorating it can easily take two. Marker pens, stickers, glitter, laminator – the options are endless. By which point it's January 3rd and I have a carefully crafted, beautifully presented set of resolutions. Eighty three per cent of which are already broken.

It's frustrating. Massively frustrating. Falling short before the Christmas tree has made it back to the loft. It's certainly not the ideal set-up for a year of high-achieving happiness. This year I'm trying something different.

After wading through the deepest darkest vaults of Facebook, in one of those three-hour click-through sessions that swallows up an entire evening without me even noticing, I found an article. A friend of a friend had posted it from a blog somewhere. It's basic premise was this – all that resolutions do is focus our minds on our struggles. It suggested that perhaps, rather than creating a long, complicated to-do list we should pick a word – a single word – to guide us through the year. That maybe a softer approach might have further-reaching, longer-lasting effects.

I believe they call it a revelation. How have I never noticed this before? That all my New Year's resolutions come from a place of 'not enough'?

Losing weight. Getting fit. Finding a job. Finding a different job. Moving house. Being nicer to the kids. Getting out more. Resolutions that I have made a hundred times. Maybe more. And all coming from not being enough. Not thin enough or fit enough. Not kind enough or loved enough or successful enough. No wonder the motivation has disappeared long before the Christmas tree. Resolutions are basically a glitter-encrusted, colour-coded list of all the ways that I think I'm failing. If I start my year, or even my day like that, it will never end well. That's the voice of experience talking.

So this year I'm trying the Internet's advice. Picking one word to guide me through the year. One single word. For twelve months. That's tricky. Especially for me. I love words. I thought about it for a long time. Apparently you should do that. And I surprised myself.

My word for this year? Gentle.

Gentle.

It's not exciting. Or dramatic. Or bold. It looks weird if you write it often enough. If you search Google images you mostly get soft-focus pictures of kittens and butterflies and tiny baby birds. It's not the kick-ass kind of word I hoped for. But it might just be right.

This year I will be guided by gentleness. At least, that's the plan. In theory.

This year I will absolutely definitely try to be gentle. That's probably more realistic.

Gentle with myself. When I'm tired and grumpy. When I'm not making my recovery as quickly as I'd like. When I've watched too much television, or gone to bed too late, or eaten nothing but cake for a week. Gentle.

Gentle with the children. When they've been up four times in the night. When they want my attention and I'd rather be doing something else. When they're acting up because they're tired, or worried, or three years old. On the days when I wish I'd just gone back to work. Gentle.

Gentle with Wes. When he calls me from a quiet hotel room while I'm fighting the children into bed. When he needs his own space – to think, or plan, or build a workshop. On the days when we're both too tired for civil conversation. Gentle.

It has potential. It could work. The really great news is, I can still spend three days making a pretty sign. The difference being that this time round I might actually feel better for looking at it.

Result. Now, where did I put that glitter?

Brightening up.

My Nan has a way with words. She's full of stories about the 'nippers' along her road, the 'dancing queen' downstairs and the entertainers at her old-age club, who are 'gay – but they do sing really nicely'. If she wasn't eighty-something and practically blind she'd get herself into a lot of trouble. Either that or she'd be working for UKIP.

Her trademark is a half-sigh, followed by the pronouncement that at least 'It's not as bad as it could have been'. Which is fine, unless she's referring to the painstakingly handcrafted birthday card you've presented her with. Or the song you've just sung. Or the name you've chosen for your child.

It's become a standard family retort. Why say outright that something's great, when you could use a backhanded-compliment-disguised-as-an-insult? Even Wes, with his upbeat, tell-it-straight South African mind-set has embraced it as an all-purpose phrase. Somehow, it just works.

The trouble comes when something genuinely is bad. It can be hard to differentiate. Difficult to know what words to use. Over the last week I've been getting worried. Very worried. That things might genuinely be bad. Again. Inside my head.

I've worked myself into a frenzy over the upcoming return to normality. The New Year. The end of the Christmas holidays. The needing-to-function-on-my-own. I've convinced myself that there's no way I'll be able to make dinner with two small children around. Despite the fact that I managed it last year. I've convinced myself that I'll never write again. That I've lost any skill I ever had. That somehow the simple change of calendars has drained all my creativity and all my resolve. That when Wes goes back to work and real life rears its big, ugly head, I won't be able to cope.

Wes has been worried too. Veering between hugs, pep talks and baking treacle tart. Perhaps I should panic more often.

When yesterday dawned, January 6th, I was nervous. To say the least. Apparently it's statistically the most depressing day of the year. Even if you're in peak mental health. I didn't fancy my chances.

Wes left the house at 6 a.m. The children were up at 7. And, miraculously, they were happy. Smiling. Not screaming, or shouting, or stamping their feet. For the first time in weeks. I have literally no idea why. But it's amazing what a difference it can make.

Just as well. By lunchtime there were nine of us. A combination of cancelled doctors' appointments, overcrowded soft play centres and not-yet-reopened toddler groups saw two mums, two pre-school girls and two toddler boys join the three of us in our kitchen for sandwiches and leftover treacle tart.

There weren't enough chairs. The girls ate their lunch on a picnic blanket, squeezed between the back door and the washing machine. I cut the bread with my usual level of skill. Which meant that most of the sandwiches had holes in. Joel spent an hour eating post-lunch scraps. Straight from the floor.

It was chaos. But somehow, it wasn't stressful. Not at all. It was wonderful.

Afterwards Joel napped, Elvie drew twenty-seven entirely yellow pictures and I decided to stay true to my year-of-gentleness by dozing on the sofa before making dinner. Which consisted entirely of moving beige-coloured, pre-prepared foodstuffs from the freezer to the oven to the plate.

Wes arrived home that evening to actual laughter. For the first time in months. Maybe years. Elvie blowing bubbles in the bath, and Joel running naked through the hallway. Turns out gentle can be fun.

Later we compared days over a cup of tea. In true Nan style, I assessed mine as being 'Not as bad as it could have been'. Somehow that doesn't seem right. Not today. I'm a Grade-A expert at the terrible British art of playing-things-down. But sometimes even I need to admit that I had a good day. That we had fun. That the children enjoyed themselves. That everyone went to bed happy.

I know why I'm scared to be positive. It's the awful, stifling fear that if anything positive happens, there must be untold horrors waiting around the corner to keep the stars aligned. There's no logic to it. But it feels real. Very real. It's suffocating.

I don't want Wes to be surprised when he comes home to happiness. I don't want my children to be surprised when I say 'yes'. I don't want to be surprised every time I have a good day. I'd like it to come more naturally. I really would.

Perhaps I need another lesson from my Nan, and another of her failsafe sayings. Which she brings out whenever the rain pauses to catch its breath. 'Ooh look ... it's brightening up.'

Brightening up.

It might just be, Nan. It might just be.

Calm is not a destination.

I've had the same bracelet on my wrist for the last seven and a half years. I've worn it in the shower. And the sea. On my wedding day. On flights around the world. And to Tesco. In labour with both my babies. At work. On nights out. Every. Single. Day.

It's nothing fancy. Just a black string with some little wooden beads. It's not a religious relic, or a lucky charm. It wouldn't make it to the table at the Antiques Roadshow. But for me, it's been invaluable. A symbol of calm. A reminder that I can, in fact, do hard things. That there was a time when my soul was at peace.

This week I cut it off.

The bracelet came from Costa Rica. It was made by the women of Estibrawpa, a remote rural tribe. The kind of people that you can only visit after a bus ride, a dug-out boat trip and a hike. The community that I called home for a month during my drama-school days. Running theatre workshops with the children. Living in the heart of the village. And escaping at the weekends to a coastal town with restaurants, internet cafes and bars playing reggae on a continuous loop.

I bought the bracelet just before we left. And I've worn it ever since. Figuring that if I can wash my clothes in the river, make porridge with a stick over an open fire and share ice-cold showers with oversized frogs, all whilst speaking nothing but Spanish, then I really can do anything.

In hard times, I've run the beads through my fingers. Over and over. Willing myself to be brave again. Trying to transport myself back to the shoeless, free-spirited, empowered, slightly sunburnt hippie that got off the plane at Heathrow. Trying to recapture that calm. Recently, it hasn't worked.

Over Christmas, I finally realised why. Calm is not a destination. It's not a fixed point on the horizon, taunting you with its distance and its proximity. Peace doesn't stay in one place. It can't. Thank goodness.

There were challenges in the jungle. Plenty of them. It was a completely different world, but it suited me perfectly. Dramatic storms. Beautiful sunshine. Great friends and amazing children. An entire month out of life when all I had to do was prepare lessons, deliver them and then try to create something edible out of the ramshackle assortment of tins and biscuits that we'd been left there with.

I had no responsibilities. Young, free and single. No house to keep, no babies to raise. No doctors' appointments or therapy sessions or antidepressants. Just me, my friends and the river. And the occasional close encounter with a machete-wielding hitman.

Nearly eight years later, life looks very different. As it should. And yet I'm still searching for calm in exactly the same place. Still aching for my month in the jungle. Knowing that if I could just be back there I'd be calm. I'd be peaceful. I'd be better.

In reality, even in the depths of the rainforest, I'd still be me. I'd still have depression. I'd still have two small children and bills that need to be paid. That month in paradise was a moment in time. And it can never be recaptured.

I'm only just working that out. Trying to stop clinging to

those memories as my only chance for peace. Realising that if I'm going to *feel* calm in everyday life, I need to find a way to *be* calm in everyday life. Real life. Right here.

And then there was Christmas.

As part of my great-Christmas-slowdown, I spent most evenings curled on the sofa with a blanket, a cup of tea and some festive telly. Often I would sit in the dark. Just the tree lights on. Little twinkling points of red and blue and green. The longer I stared at them, the calmer I became. I felt safe. Secure. Transported. Back to my childhood Christmases, when I would spend hours in the dark. Just the tree lights on.

Those lights helped me survive December without a nervous breakdown. Gave me space to think. And, eventually, the space to stop thinking and just breathe.

When January arrived, we had a tidy up/attempted to decorate/put cupboard locks on the entire kitchen so that you swear in frustration every time you open a drawer. The usual. Wes spent a while sorting out our room, and eventually hit on something of a master plan.

When he called me upstairs later, there were Christmas lights. All round our mirror. So that every night, as I go to bed, I can sit in the dark. Just the tree lights on. And think. And stop thinking. And breathe.

A little tiny piece of calm. In the midst of it all. One that doesn't leave me riddled with guilt for the far-flung adventures I'm no longer having. Or nostalgic for a time when I had fewer responsibilities. Tiny little lights. The kind of calm that will, hopefully, work for where I am right now. Which might be the only way that calm ever really works. Right here. Right now.

I'm not completely at peace. Not anymore. Not like I was in the jungle. I might never feel that way again. But I've found a way to snatch moments, however fleeting. In the midst of the chaos.

It won't work forever. That's okay. Times change. I'll change. I hope. I'm also hoping that, if I try hard enough, I'll be able to find peace anywhere. Somehow.

The Christmas boxes will always be the very first place I look.

Beans on toast.

I am, for want of a more politically-correct term, something of a kook-magnet. A disproportionate number of my stories begin with the words, 'So I met this person today ...'

Cue the old lady who asked me to pretend I was going shopping with her, in case her husband saw her and was cross. Because she shouldn't be out by herself. Due to her tendency to stop breathing.

Or the time a blue-haired woman in Morrisons talked me through the entirety of her forty-year choral history. As a result of my briefly expressed interest in the *Frozen* soundtrack.

Or the twenty-minute bus ride I spent chatting to a man who was utterly convinced that I was a surgeon. Called Caroline. Despite my protestations to the contrary.

No matter where I go, if there's anyone even remotely off-kilter, they'll find me. It's a family trait. I like to think that it proves our open-mindedness and general friendly nature. In reality, it probably means we shouldn't smile at quite so many strangers.

Last night was a prime example. After church, waiting at the bus stop. Evening drawing in. Dark. Cold. Joel in the buggy, pulling off his wellies and refusing to put them back on. Elvie sitting in the bus shelter, singing the *Swashbuckle* theme tune at the top of her lungs.

Along come two guys. Older. At a guess I'd say early

sixties. One's on the phone. Grey haired, talking a little too loud, falling off the kerb. Smelling of the pub. His friend sits on the pavement, roots through the shopping bags, and cracks open a can of lager.

Two minutes later Elvie is regaling them with tales of how Rudolph really did eat all the carrots we left out for him, and Mr Lager-On-The-Floor is asking us all to smell his new purchase. A lemon-meringue scented candle. In his defence, it was amazing. Elvie actually wanted to eat it.

Mr Grey-Hair told us that he needs the candles because he lives on a boat, and otherwise all he can smell is the woodburner. That his sister has two boys. That he would have loved children of his own, but doesn't have any.

There was a lull in conversation. Elvie resorted to her favourite question. 'What's for dinner?'

'Beans on toast.'

Followed, immediately, by shame. Because, even though Wes is away, even though I was up for three hours in the night with a sleep-resistant toddler, even though dinnertime itself would be long gone by the time we made it home, I still felt guilty.

Guilty for taking the easy route. For not having prepared a rainbow-coloured, nutritionally balanced culinary delight in the slow cooker earlier. For not being that imaginary, non-existent 'perfect' mother.

Mr Grey-Hair overheard, turned to me and beamed. His exact words were as follows:

'Wow. You must be a great cook. That's my favourite.'

We said goodbye to our new friends as they boarded their bus, and waved them off into the remainder of their lemon-meringue-scented evening. And then we went home, took off our coats and sat down to eat our beans on toast.

The kids were tired and cranky and hungry. But I didn't mind. Not too much.

Dinner felt different now. Thanks to my kook-magnetry. Thanks to our new friend and his mildly inebriated enthusiasm.

It wasn't just a plate of hastily thrown-together carbs. It was a meal. A perfectly edible one. In my own house. With my own children.

Mr Grey-Hair would have loved it.

Thanks to him, so did I.

Being there.

For the last week, Elvie has been sleeping on a sofa-bed in the lounge, while we paint her bedroom. She'll be there for the foreseeable future. Decorating with two small children is surprisingly time-consuming.

Her excitement over her 'new room' is palpable. She's told her nursery teachers, the toddler group leaders and all her friends. She's almost as excited as I am. Just the thought of being able to curl up on the sofa again in the evenings makes me giddy. I can't wait.

Despite her enthusiasm, it would seem that sleeping downstairs is, in fact, a bit scary. The room is bigger. The shadows are different. And bedtime takes longer. Much longer.

She has her nightlight. Her clock. The second-hand purple teddy bear that she can't sleep without. We count stars on the ceiling. Sing Christmas carols. Read a story. Say our prayers. Hold hands in the dark for a while. Faff about with tissues and water and Vicks until my patience wears out.

Last night I decided to use the time wisely. Have a little heart to heart. And so, as we snuggled up on her duvet, I asked what her favourite part of the day had been.

'Going to the toilet at church.' No hesitation. That may be the dictionary definition of easily pleased.

Next, I asked if there had been anything that she hadn't enjoyed. Goodness knows she had plenty of options.

Missing the bus into town because Joel was inconsolable after his nap. Watching the guy outside the community centre hurling his hangover into the bushes. Having beans on toast for dinner. Again. Getting to the snack table after all the good biscuits had gone. Seeing a man almost drown after he jumped into the swollen river to rescue his friend's dog. Me, overbalancing the buggy, so that she fell headfirst on the floor.

It's safe to say we've had better days.

'I didn't like it when I came downstairs from crèche and you weren't there, and it felt like nobody wanted me.'

Oh. Ouch. I did not see that coming.

I kept it together long enough to apologise. To explain that I'd been chatting and hadn't noticed her come downstairs. To kiss her and hold her and snuggle her into her duvet. To reassure her that next time, I'll be there. And then I went upstairs to roll into my traditional ball of miserable guilt.

Until I realised.

She wasn't sad because of all the things that I'd forgotten to do. Or how tired I'd been. Or how cross I'd got when I'd changed three stinking nappies, been poked in the eye with a plastic tiara and had my secret stash of sweets raided. All before 9 a.m.

She'd already forgotten about the biscuits. Forgotten about the toppled-over buggy. Forgotten about the near-drowning and the vomiting man, and missing the bus.

Because I'd been there. To find a different snack. To pick her up off the floor. To explain, or apologise, or put her in the buggy and walk into town instead. And that mattered.

Last week was hard. This week is no different. Tears and tantrums and meltdowns. Me and the children. Depression is digging its spiky little claws into my brain again. Whispering its nonsense into my ears. Telling me that I'm letting everyone down. Making everyone's lives more difficult. That I'm not good enough. At anything.

And then there's Elvie. My beautiful little gift. My wild, crazy, wonderful bundle of quirk. Telling me that actually, all she needs is for me to be there. With her. Holding her hand. That in reality, the most important thing I can do is show up. Every day. After every tantrum. However I'm feeling. Whatever kind of day we've had.

Be there. Show my face. Listen. Let her know that somebody wants her. Loves her. So very, very much.

The rest is extra. Decoration. We'll get there. Eventually. Perhaps.

For now. We're here. Together. Incredibly, it looks like that's enough.

February

Eaten by monsters.

Elvie is a bright spark. There's no two ways about it. Three years old and already she can teach you the colours of the various planets of the solar system, how the movement of the earth's plates creates volcanoes, and where to look for fossils. I blame CBeebies. If by blame, you mean applaud wholeheartedly whilst sighing in gratitude. Which I do. Obviously.

Nothing gets past her. Those little ears are listening. All the time. It may look like she's enthralled in her Duplo at the other end of the room, but she'll repeat your conversation verbatim over dinner. Three hours later. Whatever the topic.

I love that about her. Her keenness. Her incredible memory, Her desperate thirst for knowledge. It delights me. Having said that, I could happily have done without it this year. Done without the way she studies me, and every detail of my behaviour. Without the questions in her eyes whenever I lose my temper. Without her impatience and her anger whenever I need to rest. I can't count the number of times I've wished that she was less insightful. Less emotionally aware. Less bothered.

I know they're all wonderful traits for a little girl to have. I know I should be grateful. But I've seen what my depression has done to her. It's been a long, hard journey.

I've watched my precious girl shut herself down into a scared, angry muddle. I've lost the ability to explain the situation, or make it better. For myself, let alone her. For someone who deals in words, it's surprising how elusive I've found them to be. The right ones, anyway. Goodness knows I've used all the others.

So imagine my delight on discovering, through the parallel universe that is Twitter, a book that could solve my problems. I love books. And problem-solving. Perfect.

It's called *A Monster Ate My Mum.* And it's a children's book. Written by Jen Faulkner, herself a survivor of post-natal depression. Explaining an unexplainable illness, from the perspective of the children affected. In rhyme. With pictures. I offered to take a copy off her hands. To read, and share with Elvie, and review. You're welcome. I do what I can.

When the book arrived I decided to proof-read it before showing it to Elvie. I read it twice. Let's just say, I was not adequately prepared. It's tough to see your innermost feelings on a page. In rhyme. With monsters. I fought it for a few days and eventually did what any self-respecting professional book reviewer would do. Stuffed it down the side of my bed. And left it there. For a month.

At some point in mid-January, I had a good week. Coping really well, even though Wes was away. Getting out lots. Socialising. Enjoying the children. I dared to think that maybe, just maybe, I was better. Properly better. For good. That I should probably just send the book back, because I wouldn't be needing it. All those monsters would soon be nothing but a distant memory.

And then I crashed. It's possible that I should have seen that coming.

I was exhausted, angry and crying. I had a meltdown over our unbearably slow decorating schedule, and then sat sobbing in my bed because I didn't want to be this person anymore. There's a lesson in there somewhere. Something about pride, and falls. And unfinished book reviews.

In truth, I was scared of the book. Of the conversations it would create. Until one day, in the midst of yet-another-game-of-doctors, Elvie brought a doll to Wes and diagnosed it as 'umpressed'. He asked her what that meant, and she told him that dolly was sad. All the time.

Told you. Nothing gets past her.

Even I realised that there was a conversation that needed to happen. Soon. So I summoned up every ounce of courage I could muster. And ignored the subject completely for a few more days.

It's hard to ignore it when you're in the pharmacy. With the children. Picking up your medication. After you've dealt with Elvie's raging disappointment over the fact that we have absolutely not come in to buy lollipops. I told her that we were collecting Mummy's medicine. She asked me what it was for.

Deep breath. Look her in the eyes.

'You know that sometimes Mummy gets really tired and sad and a bit grumpy?

'Yep.'

No hesitation. Not even for a second. Bright she may be, tactful she's not.

'Well, the medicine is to help me feel better. So that I'm not so tired all the time. And I'm not so grumpy. Or sad.'

I told her that my sadness was called depression. And that I had a special book for her. To help her understand. That we would read it at bedtime. When Joel was asleep. Just the two of us.

And so we did. I read it. And she listened. She heard about the brave boy. And the monsters who had stolen parts of his mum. Her laugh, her smile, her spark. She heard that none of it was the brave boy's fault. That the monsters were sorry. That everything would be put right, eventually.

Afterwards, I asked her what she thought. Apparently she was scared of the monsters. Me too, sweet girl. Me too.

We talked for a long time. About this being our special book.

About how depression makes people feel. About where, precisely, the book would be stored. That was a long conversation. Very long. In a slightly manic, I'm-processing-something-huge-and-need-to-talk-about-something-completely-unrelated-while-I-figure-it-all-out kind of way. On both our parts.

There were lots of cuddles. Lots of reassurances. Yes, I will get better. Yes, I will be here to get her up in the morning. No, the funny little misshapen star on her nightlight doesn't look like the monster from the story. No. Really. It doesn't. Please go to sleep.

Maybe it's all a bit too deep for a three year old. Even one who's absurdly emotionally aware. She adores the rhyming, corrects me already if I miss anything out, and is in love with the dreamy, abstract pictures. But I'm not sure she understands the symbolism. Not sure what connections she's making between the monsters and my illness. It's possible she's concerned that they're really out there, waiting to catch me and munch off what's left of my smile.

We might need to talk about that. But now we can. Just holding the book in my hand gave me the confidence to broach the subject. To peel away the secrecy. To bring her into the process, and into my life. Instead of always pushing her away. We have a shared language now. Some common ground. A brave little boy. His mum. Some monsters. To help me deal with my own.

We have a lot of talking still to do. A lot of explaining. A lot of reassuring. A lot of healing. But we're on our way. Finally.

Thank goodness. And thank Jen.

Sick days.

Being ill is rubbish. Full stop.

I still remember the build-up to that December, one

fateful year in primary school. My birthday was approaching, and I was, as usual, beyond excited. I used up every last one of my woodland animal stickers making party invitations. And then I got mumps and everything was cancelled.

Seriously. All the stickers. I'd even used pinking shears. Illness has no respect for my creative flair.

It's hard to be ill as a kid. Partly because you don't really have a clue what's happening. Which adds an element of jeopardy for everyone.

I spent most of the weekend holding a bucket in front of Elvie's face, because she was convinced that she was about to be sick. Except that she wasn't. In my personal experience, small children rarely ever actually know that they're going to throw up. Until after they've projectile vomited over at least two sets of clothes, bedding or family friends.

It's hard to be ill as a kid. But it does have its advantages.

Afternoons curled up on the sofa under a blanket. Drinking Ribena and watching *The Sound of Music* on VHS. New colouring books and pens. Treats, cuddles and flat lemonade. With a straw. Occasionally even a video camera snuck in to capture your feverish, faintly delirious musical outbursts. No? Yeah, me neither. Whatever.

It's a shame that sick parents don't get the same perks. A real shame.

For the last ten days our little family has been a breeding ground for flu, bronchitis, tracheitis and teething-related woes. With some almost-broken ribs thrown in for a laugh. It has not been a happy house. Although it's probably been a record week for the local pharmacy.

I've made breakfast through gritted teeth and tears of anger and just-wanting-to-be-tucked-up-in-bed-with-some-ibuprofen. Whilst the children wailed because their toast didn't arrive quickly enough.

Wes and I have spent a lot of time silently sizing each

other up. To see who has the most serious diagnosis, at any given point. Who should be making the lunch? Who's up to the nursery run? Who can fall asleep first?

I've crawled into bed, fighting through a migraine, medicated up to my eyeballs. And then had to drag myself out again because Elvie is screaming the house down and only Mummy will do.

I've shared my bed with a snotty, snoring toddler and a wriggly, long-limbed pre-schooler. When all I wanted was space. And peace. And quiet.

I've coughed and spluttered and sweated and shivered my way through the week in a haze of paracetamol. And boy, have I been grumpy about it.

Some people deal with sickness really well. They have endless patience when their children are ill. They cope admirably with disrupted sleep. They manage to be loving and giving, even in the midst of their own searing pain. I am not one of those people. Not even slightly.

I get cross and tired and take it all very personally. I spend most of my time berating the unfairness of a world in which I am not allowed to just hide in my bed and feel sorry for myself. Which obviously puts me in the best frame of mind for recovery. Positive thinking and all that.

It's times like this when I suspect, somewhere deep in my heart, that I was not designed for motherhood. I'm really bad at the whole selflessness thing. Which is a pretty big part of the deal.

And then, in the middle of the night, something happens.

Joel wakes up. Crying. Not so much because he's ill. Just because he's sad, and he needs some comfort. I'm getting ready for bed. Grumpily. Wes is changing our bedding again in a last-ditch attempt to drive out the germs, once and for all.

Joel won't settle himself, so Wes goes in, picks him up, hugs him. Still crying. He carries him into the bathroom. Still crying. And then he sees me. He reaches out his chubby little toddler arms, and I lean over to take him. Snuggle him close. And he's quiet. Instantly. Curled up in my arms. Just like he did when he was brand new.

I hold him. I rock him. And he falls asleep on my lap, sitting on the bedroom floor while Wes changes the bed sheets around us.

I stayed there, cuddled up with my baby, for much longer than he needed. Soaking up the love. Drowning in the overwhelming knowledge that, in spite of everything, I was exactly the right person, in exactly the right place, at exactly the right time. And, in that instance, there was nowhere on earth I would rather have been.

Parenting is tough. Parenting while you're ill is hideous. But being a parent is a gift. Treasure wrapped in snotty tissues.

I'll take it. Even on the sick days.

Feasting and famine. And everything in between.

I'm an all-or-nothing person. Which is annoying.

It means that ten minutes after *The Great British Sewing Bee* finishes, I'm wondering how to find time in my schedule to hand-sew the children's entire wardrobes. Rather than actually finishing the alterations to Elvie's curtains.

It means that I want to write every day. Preferably three times a day. That I get frustrated when I only have the time and energy to do it once a week. If I'm lucky. It means that I buy a new lipstick, and don't wear it. Because I don't have a new image, career and personality to go with it.

It's an exhausting way to live. But I can cope. Mostly. Provided that the rest of my life is on an even keel.

Ha.

Our family is not easily described as normal. The concept of 9-5 is not one that we're familiar with. Wes is self-employed and goes wherever the work is, whenever it's available. Often he'll turn up at a venue in the early hours of the morning with no idea what he's going to be working on. Those are the days that he texts me saying that Emma Thompson has just arrived for a press conference. Or that he's sharing a stage with the Jersey Boys.

He loves his work. He's brilliant at it. And it definitely has its advantages. I'm lucky enough to have a husband who can craft a functional dining table in half an hour. Or pull together a garden bench from leftover pallets, for a party. He's just built a beautiful cabin bed for Elvie. We have a store-room full of timber, paint and perfume. All salvaged from various different jobs. Just waiting to be used.

There's just one problem. For me, at least. That even keel I was looking for? It's not much good for that. I'm not the only part of this family that's all-or-nothing.

There are months in the year when Wes has so much work that we pass like ships in the night. Usually the middle of the night. Clutching a vomiting baby, or a crying child, or a handful of ibuprofen. Times when we'd forget the sound of each other's voices if it weren't for all the answerphone messages. Wondering where the remote might be, or whether he made it to Birmingham, or why I haven't returned his call yet and are we actually still alive?

Those times are great for making money. And stressful in every other possible way.

And then there are the slow months. When there are weeks without any work. No money coming in. Water bills, and a mortgage to pay. Hoping against hope that there will be a phone call with more work before the money from the busy times runs out.

Now is one of those months. The second kind. The slow ones.

I would so dearly love to be reasonable about it all. To take the same approach as Wes. The one that says we've been doing this for years and it always balances itself out eventually, so let's just calm down.

I find that hard. Really hard. Bordering on impossible.

When times are busy, I'm stressed because I'm looking after the children by myself for weeks on end and I'm losing my mind and I just need a break and how can work be so much more important than me?

When times are quiet, I'm stressed because the money is going to run out and what if he never gets any more work ever and maybe I should just set up my own business selling jam because that's the only logical solution.

Awkward.

Normally, I can cope. Just about. By which I mean that I only melt down once a week. Maybe twice. At the moment it's different. Right now, everything is too all-or-nothing, even for me. I know. It's ironic. How d'you like that, Alanis?

Elvie, who is normally so independent that you're lucky to get a cuddle, has decided she can't possibly sleep unless she's in our bed. All night. Which is adorable. Obviously. Except that I desperately need my child-free space. And I resent having to share a bed with a snoring, wriggling three year old. Who prefers the duvet to be halfway down the bed, and has a tendency to ninja-whack you in the face. With her elbows. While you're sleeping.

We've started roughly a hundred home-improvement projects in the last month. Elvie's room is half-finished. Unsurprisingly, given that the mural she requested will take up two whole walls. We're halfway through putting up a photo wall in the kitchen. I'm tripping over paints and curtain rails every time I go to bed. And the garden looks like an earthquake has ripped through a building site in the middle of a prehistoric swamp.

It's no wonder that I have been obsessively tidying shelves. In a futile attempt to maintain control over something. Anything. Even a few inanimate objects. Everything is out of place. Everything is messy. Everything feels like chaos. Which is not something that my brain enjoys. At all.

In the midst of all the soupy, swirling fog in my brain, one phrase has been stuck on repeat. 'I have learnt to be content whatever the circumstances.' It's from the Bible. Philippians 4:11 to be precise. Don't be too impressed with my encyclopaedic knowledge. I may have had some assistance. From Google.

It's one of *those* phrases. The kind where, if I ever met the guy who came out with it, I'm pretty sure I'd punch him in the face. Along with whoever decided that your 'School days are the best days of your life.' Seriously. We can all be grateful that's not true.

It's always seemed a little smug. So, you've learned the secrets of contentment. Whatever happens. Great. Good for you. Now I can add guilt-for-not-finding-all-the-answers to the delightful little hurricane that's ripping through my brain.

Not that I make snap judgements. At all.

Today I wondered whether there was more to it. Whether I had, in fact, been a little harsh. Jumped up and bitten slightly too early, in order to project all my problems onto some poor dead writer who's been gone for a few thousand years and isn't exactly able to fight back.

Today, I read the whole passage. Turns out Google really does know everything. It's Philippians 4:11-13 and it goes like this:

> ... I have learned to be content whatever the circumstances. I know what it is to be in need, and I know what it is to have plenty. I have learned the secret of being content in any and

every situation, whether well fed or hungry, whether living in plenty or want.

I know. So far, so smug. But stay with it.

... I can do everything through Him who gives me strength.

There it is. Right there.

Turns out *he* didn't have all the answers. Not by himself, anyway. It's possible he wasn't even trying to be smug. Maybe he was, genuinely, trying to help. To point the way towards something that seems completely and utterly unobtainable.

I know, beyond any shadow of a doubt, that being content in every situation would change my life. Whether there's work coming in or not. However many small children spend the night on my pillow. Whatever state the garden/kitchen/house is in.

I break my back trying to control everything. Maybe, just maybe, it's time to step back. Breathe a few deep breaths. Hand it all over to someone bigger and wiser than me. Wait for Him to give me strength. Instead of searching for it myself in a freshly-organised sock drawer.

I'm not sure how it works. But I need to try. *I can do everything through Him who gives me strength.*

I hope He's good at mending curtains.

Sewing machines, fairies and crumble. (Notes on failing.)

I got the sewing machine out today. Finally. The one my Mum loaned me. The one that she bought when I was five years old and which is now, unbelievably, classed as vintage. Apparently I am growing up, after all.

The Honest Mums' Club

I'm determined to finish Elvie's curtains. So that, fourteen months after moving in, she'll actually have some that fit her window. I've altered one already. After buying them too large, because they were cute, and cheap, and the last ones in the shop. It's hanging there smartly. Almost straight. Next to some fabric, draped over the other curtain pole. Holding space for its matching pair.

It's eight months since I finished the first one. Yes, we've been busy. Yes, I've been depressed. We've been ill and away and all sorts. More excuses than I can count. Every one of them valid.

It was only this afternoon, with a mouthful of pins and a tape measure round my neck that I faced the real reason for the slightly ridiculous delay.

I'm scared.

Scared that my high school textiles teacher was right to call me a 'plonker'. Scared that my measuring skills really are as bad as I fear, and the curtains will end up being completely different lengths. Scared that getting the first one right was a fluke. Beginner's luck. That I'll get discovered. Exposed as the fraud that I'm pretty sure I am.

It's not the first time I've had this problem. While we were dating, I made Wes an apple crumble. Apparently it was so good that he almost proposed on the spot. As a result, it was literally years before I made him another. Not because of a deep-rooted fear of marriage. Or a worldwide shortage of apples. Because I was scared that if I tried again, it would go wrong. That he'd be disappointed. That he'd find me out.

I do this all the time.

Last year, we decorated Joel's room. I painted a mural. Pirates, ships, treasure chests, sea creatures. All in varying shades of 3-for-the-price-of-1 paint testers. I love it, and I'm very proud of it. It makes me smile whenever I set foot in his room. Unless it's before 7 a.m. It's a mural, not a magic wand.

At the moment we're mid-way through decorating Elvie's room. She wanted a mural too. A fairy forest and a princess and a castle. Of course.

I love painting. Creating. Art of pretty much any kind. But the thought of another mural terrified me. Because surely now I'd be found out. Everyone would realise that I can't actually draw. That I'm not as creative as they thought. As creative as I had hoped.

Every time I've worked on it, it's taken me at least twenty minutes to get anything on the wall. Twenty minutes of agonising and fretting and working through all the worst-case scenarios. Staring at the paints. Checking Twitter. Convinced that this will be the time I mess it up. The time I blow my cover.

Now, it's almost done. All except one fairy, a princess and a little bit of grass. And some glitter. I've been putting off these finishing touches for days. Despite Elvie's constant reminders that it's not finished yet. Because somewhere, deep down inside, I still feel like a fraud. People compliment my work-in-progress and I shake my head. Because I know that they're wrong. They just haven't realised that I'm blagging this whole thing. That everything is being done on a wing and a prayer and the hope that nobody looks too closely.

I've spent most of my life being scared of failing. Terrified of being seen. Really, truly seen for who I really, truly am. Scared that any successes I might have are accidental. That underneath it all, I'm not smart/talented/fun/nice/thin/exciting enough. The list goes on. And on.

I know that it holds me back. It stops me trying new things. It means that Wes doesn't get as many desserts as he'd like. It means that often I feign disinterest to cover up the fact that I desperately want to do something and am utterly convinced that I'll fail.

Slowly, slowly, ever so slowly, I'm coming round to the possibility that failing is not the end of the world. That trying, being real and vulnerable and taking risks might be the better option. Better. Not safer. Or easier. Or less likely to keep me awake all night worrying. Unfortunately.

I always had an idea of the sort of person I would be. The sort of parent I would be. None of these ideas involved therapy, or medication, or computerised support sessions. If we're measuring against expectations, I've failed spectacularly. And repeatedly.

I'm starting again. Again. But this time round, I'm doing it in the open. Being truthful. Being seen. A public failure, if you like. And honestly, I've never had better friends. Never felt more accepted. More seen for who I really am. More loved. Less judged.

I painted a fairy onto Elvie's mural last week. I got impatient, didn't wait for the layers of paint to dry and her whole face ended up a smudgy, streaky mess. More zombie-movie-extra than small-girls-bedroom. I failed. And I wiped it off. And only swore a little bit. And started again.

Last time I made a crumble, there was something wrong with the flour. Or the butter. Or the sugar. Either way, there was nothing crumbly about it. I failed. I put it in the oven anyway. And it came out fine. Cakey, but delicious. I'm ninety per cent sure that the children's vomiting that night was unrelated.

This afternoon my slapdash approach to measurement meant that one corner of Elvie's curtain was way off. Properly wonky. I failed. And I sat in the kitchen, next to my somehow-vintage-already sewing machine, and unpicked all the stitches. And started again.

I fail. A lot. Every day. Sometimes thirty-four times. Before breakfast.

Maybe it's time I stopped trying to avoid it.

There are worse things in life than mismatched curtains. Apparently.

SPRING

March

Learning to live the life of Riley.

This weekend I stayed in a hotel. For 21 hours. All by myself.

I've not had a single night to myself since Elvie was born. Not one night where I wasn't listening for a wail. Trying to soothe a teething baby. Or dealing with night terrors. Unless you count Leicester. Which I don't. Working until 2 a.m. and then collapsing into bed. That's not a night off, not in my book.

It's safe to say that three years of almost-sleeping have taken their toll. As have two bouts of postnatal depression, 27 rounds of teething and a double dose of chicken pox. I just need a break.

Wes booked the room on my behalf. As a surprise. While he was away for a whole week with work. A week which I mostly spent sobbing into the phone. And the children's cereal. He can probably write off the expense as 'crisis management' on his tax return. Safe to say it was completely unexpected, very exciting, and ever so slightly terrifying.

Not the being-on-my-own part. I'm okay with that. I like to think I'm pretty good company. It's just that I get a little overawed by 'posh.' Always have. As teenagers, my sister and I begged my parents not to get a coffee table on the grounds that it was just too fancy. I get intimidated if you use cutlery to eat a pear. Or a pizza. Needless to say, a hotel with spa facilities, an award-winning restaurant and room service is way outside my comfort zone. Fortunately they don't have valets. I might never have made it through the door.

Thank goodness I did. My 'room' was a small apartment, thanks to a sneaky upgrade after a suitably well-spun sob-story from Wes. And suddenly, there I was; in a beautiful suite, in a lovely hotel, all by myself. More than a little scared of all the posh things.

I figured out my coping mechanism early. Stay in my suite the whole time - reading books, watching tv, and ordering room service. That way I wouldn't see anyone, nobody could throw me out for lowering the tone, and there would be way fewer chances to embarrass myself. When Wes picked me up, I could tell him that was exactly what I needed. Job done. Except. One problem. Urgh.

The problem was the book that I'd taken. *The Gifts of Imperfection* by Brené Brown. Yep. Her again. I'm not on commission. I promise. She says I should lean in to uncomfortable feelings. Not avoid them. In order to actually feel something. Anything. Rather than numbing it all away. This makes a lot of sense. But it's also bloody hard.

For instance. Guest information advised that if I wanted to eat dinner in the restaurant, I should book in advance. Simple. For other people, perhaps. It took me ten minutes, one narrowly avoided panic attack and a lot of pointless Facebook browsing to muster up enough courage to call them. Seriously. Lean in. When I did, I was stunned that they weren't put out, or angry. They didn't ask who the hell I thought I was, wanting *them* to cook dinner for *me*. It's almost as if they're paid to do it. Crazy. Me. Not them.

One potential trauma avoided, I decided to brave the pool. I have less than no idea about hotel pool etiquette. Do I take a towel with me, or a bag, or just my swimsuit? Will there be lockers, or is it some fancy place where you just leave your clothes on the bench and trust that everyone else's are so much nicer that nobody will bother stealing yours?

Signing in, I felt like a fraud. Like my respectable-woman-in-a-hotel cover was about to be blown to bits. I was so scared of doing it 'wrong'. Whatever that looks like. Thankfully there were lockers. I could deal with that. I had the choice of cubicles or benches. So far, so good. And then I saw the sign: 'Poolside shoes must be worn.'

For the love of all that is sacred, what are 'poolside shoes'? What on earth do they look like? Where would you buy them? Are they even a thing? Enough. Stop. Lean in. I wore my flip flops, on the basis that they were the only shoes I had with me. And hoped that I wouldn't leave mud trails on the tiles.

I swam for an hour. Up and down, up and down. Unlike what usually passes for 'swimming' in our family – an hour of holding a small person in armbands, who's clinging to you for dear life while you try to persuade them that everyone's having fun. Turns out proper swimming can be very relaxing.

And so to dinner. I am, by nature, a nervous diner. Particularly in fancy restaurants. Even with Wes for backup. This time I was by myself. And wearing flip flops. The same ones I'd worn to the pool. They squelched. A lot.

When I reached the restaurant, the waitress told me there would be a thirty minute wait for food and showed me to my table. With a look that said, 'Really, you're going to wait for half an hour? By yourself?' Admittedly, I wasn't flying entirely solo. I had a very friendly glass of Amaretto.

When you eat alone, the waiting staff are lovely, and very attentive. I imagine they're trying to put you out of your misery as quickly as possible. I hadn't expected everyone else to be quite so attentive too. I got pitying looks from every woman in the restaurant. Repeatedly. One even grabbed her boyfriend's arm, so that he would turn and stare. Apparently eating by yourself is not the done thing. Imagine if they'd known about the flip flops.

My cheeks burned a little. Ok, they burned a lot. I contemplated running away. But I stayed put, leant in and ordered some food. In the end, I quite enjoyed it. Maybe it was the challenge. Maybe it was the Amaretto. Either way, I had a lovely time. Crab samosas. Duck breast with roasted peaches. And I left the restaurant feeling like a hero. The hero of my very own low-budget, niche-market, food-based movie.

I squelched back upstairs to eat some complimentary ginger biscuits, try out the hotel bathrobe and test every possible lighting combination in my suite. Man, they love switches.

I did, eventually, go to sleep. And it was wonderful. Drifting off peacefully, knowing that none of the banging doors or people's voices or creaking floorboards had anything to do with me. Not a hint of the heart-stopping, electric-shock-instantly-awake that I get at the slightest noise from my babies. I told my therapist that anxiety isn't much of an issue anymore. It's possible that I need to reconsider.

When I eventually woke up, there was a Saturday paper outside my door, and a hot breakfast delivered soon after. To my room. Under a cloche. There are no words.

I don't remember the last time I felt so spoilt. To be honest, I don't remember the last time I ate two meals in a row by myself. I didn't even feel the slightest pang of guilt. None at all. Which is saying a lot. I can usually be relied on to feel guilty about pretty much anything.

All that reading and eating and leaning in has left its mark. I'm still staggered that it worked. That nobody rumbled me. That, in fact, there wasn't anything to rumble. That perhaps I deserve to be treated just as well as anybody else. I might need to sit with that for a while.

It's been a big day for me and my soggy flip flops.

I'm looking forward to the next time already.

10 reasons why parenting is *exactly* like being a student.

Student life: carefree, master of your destiny, expert user of the 'emergency fiver' function on the electricity key. Bliss.

If those glorious years of freedom are still fresh in your memory, parenting can come as a nasty shock. Fear not. Scratch the surface (not literally, unless you're wearing protective gloves), and it's all uncannily familiar.

1. High maintenance housemates

Nightmare. Leaving great clumps of hair in the shower, and piles of unwashed dishes on the side. They remain entirely oblivious to their share of the gas bill, they borrow your toothbrush and are conveniently blind to the gentle prodding of the post-it note messages stuck to every surface. Draining your energy with their endless drama and eternal woe-is-me attitude.

Consider it boot camp. There's no colour-coded rota or excruciatingly tense house meeting that can tame a toddler who has decided to decorate the floor with his dinner. On a positive note, he will be more than happy to clean his toys. In the dishwasher.

2. Procrastination

As a student it's entirely possible to get to the end of the day without achieving anything. At all. Unless you count getting up before midday, inventing a new sandwich and watching *Doctors.* Which apparently, most people don't. More fool them.

Parenting occupies exactly the same space within time's great Bermuda Triangle. You haven't sat down all day. The house is littered with cups of tea that you haven't had time to finish. And yet somehow, the lounge is messier than it was this morning, nothing on your to-do-list is done and the laundry pile has quite literally exploded.

I've developed a cunning strategy to overcome this particular problem - wait until the pre-schooler is at nursery, and the toddler is napping. Hey presto, you're ready to take on the ... ooh, look, Twitter.

3. Public interest

I like to think that, as a student I got people's attention because of my eclectic outfit choices. Or the sheer amount of fun I was having. It could also have been the aura of general brilliance that seeped out of my well-cared-for pores.

Now, if people are staring, it's because it's January, it's minus-something-horrendous degrees and the children have chosen to rebel against the repressive patriarchal institution of footwear. Or perhaps because they coloured each other in. With permanent markers.

4. Judgement Day

I went to drama school. So save all your witty comments about 'soft options', or 'Mickey Mouse degrees' or 'pretending to be a tree'. Believe me, I've heard them all before. Many times. Mostly from people who are huge advocates of business courses. In response, I ask you this: how many accounting degrees run classes from nine till five, five days a week, and start each morning with an hour's warm-up run by a tiny, impossibly bendy sadist? Exactly. I didn't think so.

The truth of it is, whatever course I had taken, whichever university I had studied at, someone would made a snarky comment. It's exactly the same with motherhood. Stay at home or work? Breast or bottle? Separate rooms or co-sleeping? NCT? Dummies? Home-schooling? Fussy eaters? Second-hand shoes?

No matter what you choose, someone will disagree. Unfortunately that's a given. At times like this, it's best to follow the pre-schoolers - turn around, stick your fingers in your ears and saunter off chanting nursery rhymes until someone brings you cake. Because really, it's nobody's business but your own. And everyone loves cake.

5. All-nighters
Getting the bus home at 7 a.m. After dancing the night away, politely declining cocaine, drinking 4 a.m. milkshakes at Tinseltown and spending hours at the bus stop debating the potential benefits of inflatable sleeping bags. Before falling into bed, sleeping all day and waking up at dinnertime to bake brownies. Heaven.

Parenting? Exactly the same. If you exchange the dancing, milkshakes and enthusiastic debate for teething, night terrors and half-imagined sounds that may-or-may-not-have-been-the-baby-vomiting-in-his-cot-so-we'd-better-go-and-check. Just in case.

Oh, and swap the bed, sleep and brownies for CBeebies, caffeine and anything-that-might-have-once-touched-some-sugar. There's no getting round it. This hurts.

6. Inappropriate bodily functions
The story goes that, after my twenty-third birthday party, a course-mate-who-shall-not-be-named went back to a friend's house, wildly drunk, and pooed on her curtains.

Some things don't change.

7. 'It seemed like a good idea at the time.'
This phrase covered the majority of my student life. The hastily invented store cupboard 'cocktails'. Walking home barefoot through Soho at 3 a.m. All-you-can-eat Chinese buffets with sticky floors and dirty glasses. All embraced with

a naive youthful innocence. And all paid for afterwards. With interest.

I still use that phrase. A lot. When we throw off the toddler's schedule to hang out with friends. And reap the overtired, whinging 'rewards' for days afterwards. When we sneak off for an evening date, stay out way past bedtime and get woken at 5 a.m. by two bright-eyed little monkeys who want to play.

Or when we decided that it would be great for Santa to bring Elvie 'big girls' scissors' like the ones they use at nursery. Thankfully it was only a small chunk of hair. This time.

8. Simple eating

As a student, you develop an almost superhuman ability to survive on nothing but beans on toast. For weeks at a time. Because you're too busy, or too poor, or frankly too apathetic to bother cooking anything else.

It's a habit that sticks. Except that now, despite still being busy and poor, you're desperate to try something different. Which is tricky when your three year old has decided that she doesn't eat 'leaves', potatoes in any form whatsoever, sausages that make her 'sick like that time at Center Parcs,' or absolutely anything new. Unless it's covered in chocolate.

Beans on toast it is then. Again.

9. Pointless study

There's a moment in every student's life, usually towards the middle of your final year, when the tutors turn to you sheepishly and say, 'You know all those really important things we taught you before ... well, this is awkward, but we've changed our minds. You should probably learn these other things now.' Ah.

Parenting? Snap. Absolutely no solids until six months, until the powers-that-be decide that you should wean them at four. Co-sleeping is dangerous, unless it's the ideal scenario. 'Naughty steps' are therapy sessions just waiting to happen. Except when they work brilliantly.

And on. And on. And on.

It is perfectly feasible, whether studying or parenting, to read an entire library full of books and end up more confused than you were to start with.

Just go with it. Put the books down. Follow your instincts. Make it up a bit. Someone, somewhere, probably agrees with you. Perhaps the library doesn't stock that book. Perhaps it hasn't been written yet. Perhaps *you* should write it. Perhaps.

10. Gin
That is all.

Give it up.

I've never been a huge fan of Lent.

Maybe it's because I'm a creative. I love beautiful things. Magic. Excitement. A bit of sparkle. Forty days of quiet, miserable reflection just seems a bit much. Especially at this time of year, when the sun has barely poked its head above the horizon and we could all use some fun.

Easter is different. I love Easter. That's some serious sparkle, right there. A resurrection, angels in the garden and, at our church at least, the chance to recreate Jerusalem from cardboard boxes, branches and paint every Good Friday.

I just don't get on with Lent. I've never seen the need for a season that focuses on sadness and pain and betrayal. Alongside a bunch of friends who are ten times crankier than usual because they've given up coffee. All of them. At the same time. Whose bright idea was that?

The horrible truth is that most of us know sadness, pain

and betrayal much more closely than we'd like. We live with worries and illness and disappointment every day. No matter how much we pretend that we're fine.

This year it struck me. Maybe that's the point. Not the sacrificing of coffee or chocolate, or social media, or whatever this year's trend may be.

Perhaps the point is that we are given a solid forty days to focus on the darker areas of our lives. The sadness. The worry. The hurt. The family member who is drifting away. The career that hasn't delivered as we expected. The health problems that we can't ignore any longer. To look it all straight in the eye. The confusion. The anger. The pain.

Forty days to admit that actually, shit happens. To every single one of us, no matter how hard we pretend otherwise. And that's ok. It's normal. Maybe sometimes we need to embrace it. To sit with it. To feel it in all its gut-wrenching torturous misery before we can come out the other side.

Even Jesus wasn't fine all the time. Far from it. In the garden, he cried so hard that he was sweating blood. His closest friends betrayed him. Publicly. He was, in his very last hour, utterly forsaken by everyone. Alone. Tortured. Dead.

He gets it.

Forty days of wallowing in misery is not my cup of tea. Forty days to sit, embracing my reality in all its messiness, with someone who completely understands, might just change my life.

A life more ordinary.

I have a confession to make. For the last couple of weeks, I've felt almost like myself again. I've laughed. I've made jokes. I've bounced on the trampoline. I've said yes when Elvie begs me to get the 'arty crafty' box out. I've survived Wes's constantly changing, completely antisocial work schedule. And the extra solo parenting that comes with it.

Truth is, I've been happy. For the first time in far, far too long.

Perhaps it's the medication. My shiny little capsules of hope. Finally starting to balance out the recesses of my brain as we pass the magical six month mark.

Perhaps it's the weather. The sunshine. The earlier sunrises. Making me feel a little less alone when both children decide that they're awake at 6.20 a.m.; tired, grumpy and with remarkably little bowel control.

Perhaps it's the sleep. Elvie has finally given in to the 'star chart' approach and is sleeping through the night roughly fifty per cent of the time. Saving me from two or three bloodcurdlingly urgent middle-of-the-night dashes to her room. Every. Single. Night. Only to be confronted with a misplaced teddy bear or a slightly out-of-position duvet.

In reality, it's a combination of all those things. Coupled with the realisation that I've set my brain to work on an amazingly successful campaign of self-sabotage. For most of my adult life. And I've only just noticed.

The problem is this. Somewhere deep inside, I've always believed that I am extraordinary. Unique. Special.

There's something in the core of my being that always believed I was made for more. That nobody ever really understood me. That I was destined for incredible achievements. That frankly, ordinary life wouldn't cut it. Whatever I did, my talents were being wasted.

Whatever it was, this 'something incredible', it was always just around the corner. Tantalisingly close, whilst also being completely unobtainable. To this day, I have no idea what it would look like. A bestselling invention, or a record Oscar haul? Perhaps a Nobel prize? Or all three.

I know. It sounds ridiculous. It is ridiculous. In my

defence, Google the Enneagram. Try one of the online tests. I finally succumbed yesterday after reading about it on countless blogs and Facebook pages.

Turns out I'm a Type 4. Down to a tee. (It didn't say as much, but I'm pretty sure we're a fairly elite bunch - probably the rarest and most special of them all. Right?)

According to the description, most Type 4s identify themselves not by what they have, or who they are, but by what they're missing. Which is interesting. And, in my case at least, absolutely true.

I couldn't fully enjoy my teenage years because I was desperate for the respect and responsibility of adulthood. In my early twenties, my freedom and opportunities were tainted by the fact that I wasn't in a relationship. Then I very nearly destroyed my relationship over the fact that we weren't married. Eventually we *were* married, and all I wanted was a baby. Now, a few years into the raising of my children, I've been wallowing in the depths of depression, feeling as though all this stay-at-home-mum business is holding up my chance at real life.

Not that I can tell you what my 'real life' would look like. It's just a vague sense of dissatisfaction, of restlessness. Of missing out on something undefined and impossible to grab onto.

I've spent thirty one years dreaming of my 'what ifs'. Of the nonspecific greatness that I'm destined for. Desperately wanting to be a wonderful wife and mother. And also a wild, undeniable success. At something. Or everything. Who knows? Turns out I've never really been present. To my friends, to my family, to my husband. Not even to myself.

There's a Russian proverb that says 'If you chase two rabbits, you won't catch either.' They know their stuff, these Russians.

I've spent my life chasing two rabbits. Occasionally

more. I've even caught some of them. But they've never made me happy. Not for long. Because I've always had an eye on the ones that got away.

When I left London, a friend took me aside and made me promise not to end up as a 'boring little housewife'. I laughed. As if. I had bigger fish to fry. Lives to change. Plans to make. A whole world to win over. Hoping that maybe, one day, I'd reach a place where I was satisfied. Where I had done enough.

I know now. That time will never come. There will always be someone who is more successful than me. There will always be someone who has achieved more, with less effort, or nicer shoes. I won't ever reach what I'm missing. I don't even know what it is.

But I know what I have. Here. Now. Right in front of me.

An incredible husband. A little house of our own. Two little lovelies.

I know that, for now, I have the chance to love my family. To raise our little ones. To play with them. To read to them and make them laugh. To make our home beautiful. To shop as cunningly as possible, so that we can afford an occasional treat. To be a good friend to the people I have around me. To live the life that I find myself in. Right here. Right now.

In a few years' time, the children will both be at school. All day. Maybe then I can think about a career. About aiming for greatness without letting it consume me. Maybe. If I'm ready.

For now, I'm trying to make a conscious decision, every day. To embrace my role as the 'boring little housewife'.

It won't make the news. It won't win any prizes. It probably won't even make any money.

It's a life more ordinary.

But it's my life. And I like it.

At last.

Wishing flowers.

Our house may be small, but it's very well-placed. It's toddler-walking distance from three separate parks. Two rivers. And a meadow. So that my little shoeless crazies can spend as much time outdoors as they like. Which is a lot.

As the weather starts to improve, we're outside more and more. Especially in the 'big park', which they love. Swings, a slide, a climbing frame. And sand. Lots of sand. In summer, there's a bank of wild flowers. For now it's mostly daisies. And dandelions.

I've always liked dandelions. Not when they're yellow and garish and all-up-in-your-face. When they go to seed. And suddenly they're magical. Fairy clocks. That's what we used to call them. Holding them to our faces. Blowing. Counting. Always genuinely surprised when the 'time' they told us wasn't quite right.

Elvie loves them too. But she isn't much taken with the clocks. Which is a surprise. She loves counting. And fairies. Regardless, the dandelions have been rechristened. So that now, and probably forever, we will mostly be referring to them as 'wishing flowers'.

Whenever we see one, she stops. Picks it. Blows it. Screws her face up and makes her wish. It's adorable. Unless we're running late. In which case it's excruciating. I always ask her what she's wished for, and she always tells me. Blissfully unaware that a shared wish never comes true. Perhaps I should tell her. One day.

That scrunched up little face always wishes for the same thing. 'Fairies and princesses on my wall'. Which is cute. Except that she already has them. Thanks to her remarkably precise instructions during the last few months of mural painting.

Initially, those wishes wound me up. Back when the fairies weren't quite finished. It felt like a guilt trip, all packaged up neatly in a dying flower. Passive-aggression of the highest order. Like mother like daughter.

The mural's done now. And still, every dandelion brings the same wish. I'm starting to see it differently. Maybe it's not a guilt trip after all. Maybe it's the beauty of being three years old and content. That the greatest, most extravagant thing she can dream up is something she already has. I envy her that.

Depression is hard. It's illogical. I have weeks of thinking that I'm recovering, followed by a crash back to rock-bottom. A good month, and then a massive blip. With no logical explanation. Which is frustrating. I'm not a fan of huge amounts of effort and no discernible reward.

It's so difficult, from inside these lows, to feel positive. To feel anything, other than anger and frustration. At myself, and this stupid illness. And the world in general. I spend my days wishing for the seemingly unattainable - being better, being drug-free, being happy.

There's something in the way that Elvie uses those wishing flowers. A lesson in contentment. Or an attempt at it, at least. An attempt to find peace with myself and the topsy-turvy, one-step-forwards-two-steps-back pace of my recovery.

I don't want to stop wishing. Not at all. I just want to wish like a three year old. Make my wishes a little smaller. A little more down to earth. A little more already-in-existence.

I will wish for medication that works. For supportive family and friends. For a safe, beautiful home in which to work all my problems out.

Because I have all of those things. Already. Even on the bad days. The real beauty of it? It doesn't matter if I tell you what I've wished for. Because it's already here.

I hope there are plenty of dandelions left at the park. We'll be needing a few.

April

Impossible is everything.

The word 'impossible' is redundant. Apparently. It should no longer grace our vocabularies. Everyone from sportswear manufacturers to credit card companies would have us believe that impossible is nothing. Irrelevant. Two letters too long.

I'm sure they have a point. Of sorts. It probably boosts their sales. But I don't believe it. Not at all.

Some things are impossible. Fact.

Not in a whingey pre-schooler, 'I can't do it, it's impossible – Muuuuuuuuuuum!' kind of way. Properly, physically impossible.

It is physically impossible for me to be the Queen of England. Or President of the United States. Not that I mind.

It was impossible to cure the cancer that stole my great-uncle last year. It's impossible to bring him back. That, I do mind.

Some things just cannot be done. These days, that is a pretty radical statement.

Like most of my generation, I was brought up believing that anything is possible. That I can be whoever I want. Do whatever I want. Achieve whatever I want. So long as I put together a good, solid plan and I make enough effort, the world is my oyster.

I'm sure that the teachers, and parents, and Sunday School leaders who told me these things believed that they were doing me a favour. Encouraging me to reach my potential. Letting me shoot for the stars.

There's no such word as can't. Allegedly.

Except that, in fact, there is.

Imagine if everything *was* possible. How would you even begin to narrow down your options? How could you ever avoid the sinking feeling of failure when you're only accomplishing twelve remarkable feats a day?

Why shouldn't I try to do everything by myself? What would be the point of community? Faith? God?

If all it took was a well-thought-out plan and some fierce self-discipline, we'd work our own miracles. Every day. We'd heal ourselves. We'd save ourselves. Easter would be utterly pointless.

Lent seems like a good time to face facts. That actually, as human beings, we have limits. Some things are just impossible.

For me, anyway.

It's impossible to be entirely perfect. It's impossible to forgive every single mistake of each and every single person in the history of time through one single act. It's impossible to die a horrific, gruesome death, be stone-cold dead for three days and rise up again on Sunday morning.

At Easter, impossible is everything. Thank God.

Otherwise Jesus was just a nice guy with a good, solid plan.

Heaven forbid.

These things I love.

Some people apologise for everything. I'm one of them. Sorry.

I'll apologise if it's raining, or the council raise your taxes. Or if your picnic in the forest gets delayed by the fact that finally, just as everyone is strapped into the car and you've locked the front door, Elvie announces that she's had 'a little accident' and needs an entire change of clothes. For instance.

It's not that I am deeply apologetic by nature. It's just that I want to be absolutely sure that everyone approves of everything I'm doing. All the time. I'm not great at trusting my own judgement. Or even knowing what I want, without a light in the sky or a glowing response or a nod of approval from whoever happens to be passing.

I believe the official term is 'people pleaser.' It says a lot about me that I breathed a huge sigh of relief the first time I heard that phrase. Because, however annoying it may be, at least it's a recognised condition, so nobody can think too badly of me.

I know. I need help.

There's never been a shortage of people to please. Teachers. Parents. Lecturers. Colleagues. Bosses. The list is endless. Always waiting to give me a gold star or a good report. All told, I've done pretty well.

But for almost four years now, I've been a stay-at-home mum. I've dabbled in teaching weekend theatre classes, or selling cut-price cosmetics, but I've spent the majority of my time at home. With the babies. Not a line-manager, appraisal or pay-check in sight. Met, more often than not, with a glazed over look of instant disinterest whenever I'm asked that innocent, loaded question: 'So, what do you do?'

I've struggled. No grades. No promotions. No report cards. And, as a result, I've had the slow, creeping feeling that I'm letting people down. Letting myself down. Failing to fulfil my potential.

For the first time in my life I don't have an authority figure to answer to. I'm answerable only to my husband, my children and myself. Wes, who doesn't much mind what I do as long as the house remains structurally intact. Elvie and Joel who, if this week is anything to go by, will never be satisfied with anything. And me.

Answerable to myself. Myself. For once. Having to stop and think about what *I* want. What I actually want. For myself and my family.

It's new ground. Awkward, sometimes emotional, and a lot like stumbling about in the dark. Tripping over roots that have been buried deep for a long, long time.

It's been hard to find my place. To find an identity of my own. Just ask my doctor. And my pharmacist. The tablets, the therapy. All of that. My struggle written all over little green prescription tokens. Finding yourself isn't as easy as it looks. It's not all backpacks and plane tickets and a chronic lack of personal hygiene.

Being a stay-at-home mum was a conscious decision. We'd talked about it. Lots. It's what we both grew up with. And it's something that we really value. The constancy. The always-being-around. The emotional stability. Which I'm hoping will arrive eventually.

And still, despite the decision-making and the conviction, there's the guilt. The crushing weight of disappointment that someone, somewhere surely feels. The worry about what other people think of me. The fear of being far and away the greatest underachiever of my drama-school cohort. Of wasting my tuition fees. And everybody's time.

I worry that I'm dull. Boring. That I don't have anything interesting to say to my pre-children friends, because I'm knee deep in nappies and nursery runs. I'm crippled by the fear that I'm inadvertently showing Elvie that the only good place for a woman is in the home.

I'm tying myself in knots. Going over and over the possibility that, in a few years' time, I'll feel completely differently about my choices. That I'll realise I made a mistake. That I should have been out there. Achieving things. Changing lives. Blazing a feminist path. I wonder if I should have a career. I'm pretty sure I should have *something*.

I'd call it a mid-life crisis, but I'm very much hoping to live past sixty-two.

So it was like a well-timed intervention to find these words on Shauna Niequist's blog:

Pay attention to what you love, not to what you should *love.*

And breathe.

That sounds like a plan. This week I've spent every spare minute trying to work out what I actually want. It's been fun. If a little strange. Looking inside myself. Trying to remember what makes me happy. On reflection, it probably shouldn't be this hard.

I've made a list. Of course. A list of things that I love:

I love having people in my house. Feeding them. Making them happy. I love the idea of creating a 'home' - a safe haven for our children and our friends. Making things beautiful. Building memories together. And recording them. I love writing. Blogging. Building up a little community of people who understand. I'm desperate to let my creativity out in new ways. I want to learn to sew. Properly. To have a garden that grows flowers. Deliberately. Not just the ones that self-seeded from next door. A vegetable patch. Chickens.

I love the idea of my children growing up knowing where their food comes from. How to make bread and when to pull up a potato. How to alter clothes so that they fit properly, and how to light a campfire. Maybe I'm old school. Maybe I'm deluded. Maybe I've been brainwashed by the controller of BBC2.

Just the thought of all this makes me happy. In my soul. It also makes me embarrassed, and instantly apologetic. Because what kind of self-respecting modern, feminist woman has these dreams? Aren't I supposed to achieve something amazing? Shatter those glass ceilings? Not live like a reject from a 1960s commune.

And yet. Really. What more could I hope to achieve? Than being happy. Being fulfilled. Expressing my creativity. Letting my children see an alternative to the rat race. Showing them what it looks like to live when your soul is alive. When there's nothing to apologise for.

It's something of a pipe dream at the moment. I can't skip off to join a commune. Yet. We don't have the space for a goat, or the time for chickens or the money for dressmaking patterns. Slowly, slowly. That's another lesson I need to learn.

I'm doing my best. Little by little. Collecting unwanted fabric from friends. Free patterns from Pinterest. Finishing Elvie's curtains. Buying bulbs for the front garden and fruit bushes for the back. Putting myself on the waiting list for an allotment. Painting tables. Having friends over for meals. Hunting for Easter eggs in the sunshine. Baking. Reading. Taking my time.

Testing the waters. Building my confidence. And, above all, trying not to apologise for any of it.

It seems like a good time to start. Spring. Easter. Perfect for a new beginning. A life where I can follow the simple, unimpressive dreams of my heart.

In the meantime I'm setting the series link for BBC2's new allotment programme. And no, I'm not sorry. Not even a little bit.

Base camp.

It's not quite 11 a.m. Wes left for work six and a half hours ago. He won't be back until long after the children are in bed.

Since he left I've changed four nappies. Two of them revolting. Joel has alternated between hysterical laughter and flat-out-screaming-tears. With no discernible reason for either. Elvie has smeared the walls of her room with two full tubes of toothpaste. She's weed all over the floor. And taken an hour to decide that she is, in fact, getting dressed.

Some days it's all too much. It's not even lunchtime.

Obviously I'm handling it brilliantly. Not even slightly cancelling the arty-crafty session I'd promised so that I can hide on the sofa with my laptop and try to ignore their constant noise.

Ha.

Thank goodness Elvie has nursery this afternoon.

April has been full-on. Wes has worked all the hours and all the bank holidays. There's been a three-week break from nursery, and all our regular toddler groups. Three weeks? For Easter? It's practically the summer holidays. With worse weather.

I coped for a while. But the combination of bored children, tired mummy and very busy daddy rarely ends well. This month is no exception.

We've had shouting. Screaming. Complete meltdowns. Wild disobedience and a lot of 'time on the step'. I've been sitting in the corner, rocking, begging everyone to be quiet and just leave me alone. For two minutes. Please. For-the-love-of-all-that-is-sacred.

In fairness, there have been *some* nice moments. Egg trails, accidental magical mystery tours, a beautiful bonfire-lit Easter morning service and a few giggles in amongst the chaos. Elvie even picked me some flowers. From someone else's garden.

It's been hard to see the positives. When the three year old is refusing to be a decent human being, and the toddler won't be put down. It really gets on top of you. Apparently giving your children away violates the Freecycle ethics policy. Can't blame a girl for trying.

Last week I reached the point of actually-beginning-to-lose-the-plot. Which is never fun.

Thankfully I have a husband whose approach to life is slightly calmer than my own. Who can look me in the eyes, discern my barely-functional state and call base camp.

Base camp was Wes's idea. Months ago. When we tried to put our family dreams down on paper. I like putting things on paper. You might have noticed. It makes them real. With the added bonus that you can laminate or shred them at a later date. Depending on how it all works out.

He figured out, quite rightly, that our lives are chaotic. That's just how it is. And most of the time, that's ok. But sometimes it tips over. Way past the point of coping and well on the way to misery and depression and oh-dear-God-I-just-want-to-run-away.

He's better at spotting it than I am. I tend to be stuck fast in the moment and the feelings and the fear that it will absolutely definitely always be like this forever.

So we made a deal. If either of us spots a wave of impending doom, we call base camp. Which means that we retreat, intentionally, to something that feels safe and simple and sustainable. Where we cancel all our non-essential events, and spend time just being with each other, as a family. No agenda. No pressure. For as long as it takes. Until we're ready.

Sometimes that manifests itself in not getting out of our pyjamas, watching hours of telly and eating takeaways. On Sunday it looked like jogging bottoms, a roast dinner and the most enormous pile of shredding, as I tackled our non-existent filing system. Let's just say that we've kept a lot of crap. And we'll be eternally grateful that our neighbours let us use their bins while they're away.

After Sunday's base camp, things feel better. Slightly. At least I'm no longer panicking about how anyone would ever find our life insurance details if we both dropped dead tomorrow.

It'll take more than a day to leave camp. We know that. Wes has booked himself off work for all the May bank holidays. His parents are coming next weekend to help out. I've signed up for some mindfulness classes. And I'm planning to clear out our loft. Get rid of some physical clutter, in an attempt to lighten our emotional load.

We might not get out much for the next few weeks. There's a fair bit of hunkering down and hiding and being intentional that needs to happen. But we're okay. We caught it just in time. And that's a good thing. Base camp is a great place to be. It's calm and it's safe and we're all in it together.

Feel free to join us.

The Honest Mums' Club.

Mothers are an advertisers dream. Perpetually paranoid, convinced that we're doing it wrong. That our days aren't simultaneously filled, educational and serene enough. That we work too much. Or too little. That we're feeding our precious offspring all the wrong foods.

We worry that in twenty years it will be *our* children costing the NHS millions in therapy. Or dropping out of college with rock-bottom self esteem and a nasty narcotics habit.

No? Perhaps it's just me.

I doubt it.

There must be a few of us, at least. Otherwise the marketing gurus have seriously misplaced their money.

You can hardly breathe at the moment for 'must-have' gadgets, or educational apps. For tutors to help your children exceed their academic potential, or forest schools for when it all gets too much. Cookbooks full of 'family friendly' recipes that leave me convinced that mine must be the only children

172

on earth who won't eat kale, or pine nuts, or anything made of potato. Clothes that wouldn't last five minutes on either of my mud-monsters. Not that they'd ever set eyes on them in the first place, given that they cost twice our monthly food budget.

I don't think that motherhood has ever been so well-marketed. So riddled with guilt, and fear, and expectations. The list of 'new baby essentials' grows longer by the day. No wonder so many people delay having children. Or just abandon the idea altogether.

It's all nonsense. In my humble opinion, anyway. Every mother - whether they're pregnant for the first time, a new mum or a seasoned pro needs only one thing in order to survive.

Friends.

Real, honest, there-through-thick-and-thin friends. Preferably the kind who are already parents themselves. They tend not to be so horrified when the topic of 'how-close-the-baby-came-to-being-thrown-out-of-the-window-at-3am' comes up.

Last night I went to a bead party. With a room full of exactly this kind of women. This kind of friends. I may just be the luckiest girl alive.

A bead party is not like a Tupperware party. Or an Avon party. Or even an Ann Summers party. Except that the host's husband had to leave the room as soon as he arrived home because there were 'just a few more boob stories to tell'. Told you. These girls are the greatest.

They've become a tradition at our church. Bead parties, not boob stories.

It's like a baby shower. But better. And with fewer presents. All the mummies get together for an evening, to show their support for the mother-to-be. We share poems and prayers and words of wisdom. Birth stories involving cupboards and French ambulance drivers, or nameless on-call-birth-partners who left their phones on silent while they drank wine and watched telly, only to miss the entire event. And, if last night is anything to go by, a lot of sugar.

Everyone brings a bead, and throughout the evening they're threaded onto a piece of elastic. So that the new mama has a bracelet. Something physical. Tangible. To wear in labour and those hazy early days. To bite on, or run through her fingers, or use as a blunt instrument against anyone who tells her that the baby will arrive 'when it's ready'.

To remind her that she is not alone.

Those bracelets are special. Beyond words. No doubt. They have starring roles in everyone's birthing pictures. But what really makes these evenings precious are the friendships.

Last night was no exception. Nine of us, sitting in a kitchen, making ice cream sundaes. And eating them too, obviously.

I'd had a hell of a day. Week, actually. With my unruly three year old. One girl arrived off the back of three sleep-deprived teething nights. Another, four months pregnant and existing on a diet of tinned caramel and super noodles, was just pleased to have cleaned her teeth without vomiting.

We all came with baggage. Some of us almost didn't make it at all after a close-call with the traffic on one of Reading's more intricate roundabouts. But we were there. We laughed. We cried. We laughed *until* we cried. We ate way too much sugar for that time of the evening. We hunted imaginary cats who may or may not have broken in through the back door. And, through it all, we were real.

Real can be hard to find these days. But when you find it, you don't let go.

These girls have been my lifeline over the last year. My place of safety. Where it doesn't matter that I have no answers. Or that I'm wearing the same clothes for the fourth day running. Or that my daughter has just styled her own hair. With peanut butter. Because they understand.

These girls hold my secrets. When I told them I was terrified of mothering a boy, they understood. When I told them I was depressed, they cried with me, held my hands and listened. They know, they care, and they don't judge. They're amazing. Every last one of them.

We know how dark and lonely motherhood can be, and we also know its delights. We've seen each other at our very best and at our absolute worst.

We've cried together through miscarriages and broken hearts. We've cared for each other's children. We've cooked meals when new babies arrive. Most of the clothes that our little ones are wearing have already done the rounds at least twice.

Some of us have real-life sisters. Some of us don't. Some of our real-life sisters live on the other side of the world. But here, in this muddle of baby bumps, leaky boobs, caramel junkies and bone-tired eyes, is another kind of sisterhood. And it is breathtakingly beautiful.

We've christened it The Honest Mums' Club. And I am beyond privileged to be part of it.

Nobody should have to face motherhood alone. We're not built that way. Community. Sisterhood. Honesty. That, right there, is what every mother needs.

Every new mother who can barely see out of her sleep-deprived eyes. Every mum of six who can't figure out how to split herself so many ways. All the home-schoolers. All the chairwomen of the board. All the Annabel Karmel devotees. All the chips-and-beans mamas.

You don't need another gadget. You don't need a new routine. Or a tutor. Or a fancy app.

All you need is friends. Real, honest friends.

And perhaps one more ice cream sundae.

May

101 ways to ruin a blanket. Or, why I'm learning to take advice.

I have a blanket. Just the one. It's beautiful. Enormous, slightly sparkly and very, very warm.

This blanket has seen me through nights in ice-cold houses, countless sick bugs and more dark days on the sofa than I care to remember. Snuggled up inside those cosy fibres, desperately hoping that they'd transport me to a world where I had no responsibilities, and nothing to wake up for in the morning.

Like most blankets, it has a care label attached. Full of useful information. 'Dry clean only.' 'Laura Ashley.' 'Keep away from fire.'

What it doesn't say is 'keep away from three year olds who are trying to eat stolen family-size pots of cherry yoghurt under the cover of blankety darkness.' There's no warning of the damage that can be wrought by little cherry-covered fingers, or the disproportionate sense of rage that may be invoked upon the discovery of this obviously hypothetical scene.

Needless to say, the blanket is now at the dry cleaners. Where, in their expert opinion, the purple stains may or may not come off.

Furious just about covers it. Just about.

Blanket-gate is the latest in a series of incidents that have tested our patience over the last few weeks. There was the one where she smeared toothpaste all over her bedroom walls. The one where she covered Joel's hair (and by proxy the walls, the carpet and the only new pair of curtains in the house) in Sudocrem. The one where she blocked the toilet after using an entire roll of paper in one go. The one where she pinched my make-up, and proceeded to decorate herself, my dressing table, and the carpet. With bright red lipstick.

Not to mention my particular favourite. The time that she pooed on a paper plate in the corner of her room. And left it festering for hours before I discovered it at bedtime.

Add those issues to the constant mix of badgering, niggling, back-chatting and just-plain-rude, and we've had ourselves a slow-burning fuse attached to a hand grenade of parental discontent. Turns out that not-quite-four year olds have all the attitude.

It's taken me a little by surprise. Mostly because she'd only just calmed down after her terrible twos. We thought we were over the worst. Ignorance is bliss. It's only recently that I've realised that I genuinely have *no* clue what to do.

It's a tough admission. She's my daughter. My own flesh and blood. A tiny little me in so many, many ways. And I have absolutely no idea how to get through to her. Sometimes it feels as if she's completely out of control. The house definitely is.

This afternoon, while she was at nursery, I took Joel to the children's centre. For some big-sister-free play. And the brilliant family worker, who hugged me back to the land-of-the-living when I turned up on my last legs a week ago, pulled me to one side for a chat. To see how things are going. How I'm holding up. What havoc Elvie has created this time.

I like this woman. A lot. She's just the right blend of bonkers and wise. She's propped me up over the last eighteen months. With her care and her questions and her cornflour-based messy play activities.

177

I talked her through the yoghurt/blanket scenario. And how badly I'd reacted. I shared my feelings of being out of control. The steps I'm taking to put some serious discipline back into our lives. How I'm trying, and failing, to control my mood swings.

She listened. Really well. Told some stories of how tough her own kids had been. Mistakes she'd made. Empathy. She's a good one. And then she shifted her position, and looked me right in the eye.

Which could only mean one thing. Advice. Urgh.

If there's one thing I struggle with, it's advice. I'm not good at taking it. Although, ironically, I'm pretty great at giving it out. Go figure.

I don't like advice because I hate admitting that I don't, in fact, know everything. Especially when it comes to my children. I carried them. I gave birth to them. They're my responsibility. Twenty four hours a day. Nobody knows them better than me. And I'm damned if someone else is going to tell me how to raise them.

Until. Until blanket-gate. After weeks of arguing and tantrums and time-on-the-step. Until I realised the glaring truth of the situation.

I do not, in fact, know everything.

I don't know what to do with Elvie. I don't know what to do with myself. I don't know how she'll turn out. I don't know how to start seeing her strong-will as an advantage. I don't know how we'll cope until she starts school. Or when she's there.

If someone I trust, who loves me and my children, and has never been anything but good to us, offers me advice ... I'd be a fool not to take it. Or listen, at least.

I listened this afternoon. Her advice was good. Suggesting new strategies. Praising what we're already doing. Support. Encouragement. From someone further down the road. A fresh pair of eyes, That haven't been quite so full of tears lately. Or toothpaste. Or yoghurt.

Nursery finished later than usual today. When I arrived to collect Elvie, they were all in the playground. Pretending to be rockets. Oblivious to us watching over the fence.

I watched her. From a distance. Doing exactly as she was told. With huge enthusiasm and a great big smile on her face. Surrounded by her friends.

Sometimes I need a step back. A different perspective. Maybe even (whisper it) a little bit of advice.

She's not a bad girl. Not at all. We've just hit a rocky patch. Hopefully we'll come out the other side. Stronger.

For now, I'm putting the yoghurt on the top shelf.

Like a girl.

Next month there's going to be a vote. In the Church of England, of all places. One that could bring women bishops into being. For the very first time.

As an accidental Anglican, I'm enormously proud of the possibility.

I'm proud of all the women who are campaigning for the cause. Proud of all the men who support them. And proud of those men who have always disagreed, but after listening, and considering, might just change their minds.

As a woman, and the mother of a daughter, I'm absolutely horrified. Horrified that it's taken this long for a vote to be scheduled. That it was ever needed in the first place. That still, in the twenty-first century, it's so very very hard to be a woman.

I have no desire to be a bishop. None whatsoever. But what if Elvie does? How is it possible that, until now, it hasn't even been an option?

How is it possible that toy manufacturers would rather she was interested in make-up, and hairstyling and fashion shows? At the tender age of three?

It's frightening.

Elvie is not what you would call a 'typical girl.' Whatever that may be.

This weekend she made a 'remote control' out of Duplo. Apparently it controls twenty-one separate things. None of us is entirely sure what they are. She reliably informs me that she's been making these remote controls for two million years, and has a medal from the Queen. For being such a great scientist. And inventor.

Her nursery report praised her for helping to rebuild the mud kitchen, and commented on how much she loves the freedom that comes from being outside.

Over the last month she has collected worms, beetles, woodlice and goodness-knows-what-else from the garden. Made them homes, inside, and demanded that we keep them as pets.

All she wants for her birthday is a kite. And a *Frozen*-themed party, with a life-size Anna made entirely from ice. Of course.

I love that she's an explorer. A wild girl. An inventor. I love that if she had to choose her favourite TV character, she'd be hard pushed to pick between a scientist and a pirate. Both of them female.

But soon she'll be four. In September she starts school. And little by little, she'll learn how the world works.

That the only way to become a powerful woman is to live as a heartless monster. Or sleep your way to the top. Or be so hideously ugly that you are forced to devote your life to your work because nobody wants to hang out with you.

Sounds harsh, I know. But if it's on the internet, it must be true. Right?

I'm scared of Elvie getting older. Because I know how hard it is. To grow up as a girl. To follow your dreams and your beliefs, even when that makes you the loser. The outsider.

I know how hard it is to break up with the abusive boyfriend who's destroyed any confidence you'd managed to salvage from your teenage years.

I know how it feels to keep your keys and your phone in your pockets at all times, so that you can always make it home. Even if the man lurking by his motorbike steals your bag.

I know how hard it is to be surrounded by beautiful, made-up school friends when you have frumpy clothes and no idea how to use foundation.

I know how disorientating it is to be propositioned by the police officer who's been asked to help you identify your mugger. How sick-to-the-stomach you feel when his colleagues cheer him on. How frustrating it is to know that there's no point filing a complaint.

I know how easily you can feel as if you've caved in to traditional stereotypes and betrayed your feminist sisters. When all you want to do is raise your children and create a beautiful home. For now, at least.

I know how impossible it is to explain to men, any men, how back-breakingly, soul-destroyingly hard it is to be a woman. And that's from my perspective. As a white British woman. A woman of privilege.

I can't begin to imagine how hard it is for my sisters across the world. Who get shot in the head for daring to go to school. Or stoned to death for marrying someone who didn't suit their father's plan.

I have a pile of books on my shelf. Filed under 'female empowerment.' I'm keeping them there for Elvie. When she's older. And devouring them myself. Right now. Brené Brown.

Caitlin Moran. Maya Angelou. To name but a few. I'll pass them down, like treasure. I'll show her the stories coming out of #yesallwomen and #likeagirl. Teach her about the suffragettes. And the No More Page 3 campaign.

In the meantime, she'll be getting that kite. We'll keep on watching pirates, and scientists, and Always adverts. She can be my assistant-head gardener. And bring back as many homeless worms as she likes.

We're getting there. One step at a time. To that magical, far-away land where it doesn't matter in the slightest what you have between your legs.

It's been a hard fight. It's been a long fight. But we owe it to ourselves, and our daughters and our granddaughters to keep going.

We fight like girls. But one day, we'll win like girls. And the world will be a brighter place. For everyone.

Bishops included.

Leaving the field.

I'm not great at camping. To be honest, I'm not even good at camping.

I'm less about the back-to-nature and more about the if-I'm-paying-to-go-on-holiday-then-I'd-at-least-like-some-proper-walls. My parents recently spent four days in a tent on the edge of a Welsh cliff during gale force winds and rainstorms. When they returned, Mum said, 'You know what? I think I like camping.' It's possible that I was adopted.

In my defence, I've had some bad camping experiences.

Scooping water out of my tent with a mug. Before we'd even finished putting it up. Staying awake all night, clinging to the tent poles to stop them blowing away. Watching my food disappear down an impromptu river in the middle of the campsite. Waking in the morning to discover that every tent except ours had been evacuated in the night after a torrential storm.

I've even ended up in an ambulance after a panic attack midway through a camping trip. Complete with worried friends, pins and needles over my entire body and an oxygen mask that refused to do its job.

I think the real problem is England. Camping in England, at any rate. It's cold. Even in the summer. And it rains. Even in the summer.

I've managed one night in a tent with the children. There's a photograph taken the morning after. All hats and jumpers and smiles. I love how happy we look. And how you absolutely cannot tell that I had been awake all night because the temperature was zero degrees and I'd had to check every five minutes that my babies hadn't frozen to death in their sleep. Take it from me - sometimes the camera really can lie.

We'd planned a three-day camping trip. By the second night we were back in our own beds. With a roof. And actual walls. All mod cons.

I love the *idea* of tents. Waking up in the morning and wandering out in the dew. The children frolicking in the grass. Going to bed when darkness falls and waking up with the sun. It sounds idyllic.

In reality, all your clothes are damp, it's beyond cold, you didn't get to sleep until 2 a.m. because you could hear every word of the neighbouring tent's all-night party, and the toilets are horrid. If there are any.

This year has been all about the gentleness. The self-awareness. Taking things slowly. Trying to accept myself as I actually, really am. Weaknesses, foibles and all.

Taking all that into account you would think that, when I booked us in for church camp, I would have had a stern word with myself and realised that I was never going to survive two nights in a tent. That perhaps I should sign myself up as a day visitor. Own my character traits and go with them. Live according to who I am, and not who I think I *should* be.

It turns out that I'm still learning. Which is why, after a week of stress, frantic packing and pointless tearful arguments, I found myself crying on the floor of our tent. At 9 p.m., on the first night of camp. Ugly, snotty crying. Like the world was about to end.

I warned you. I'm really bad at camping.

Wes took me home. Straight away. I put myself to bed, and didn't get dressed again for another two days. Days that I mostly spent sleeping and staring into space. Trying to figure out what had just happened to me. How I'd managed to break down so very thoroughly.

In fairness, it wasn't just the tent. I'd been heading for a crash for a while. Life under canvas was just the final straw. That, and the rain, and the suddenly incontinent child.

Either way, I spent the weekend in a haze of guilt. For letting everyone down. For leaving Wes with the children. Who have obviously been scarred for life by my tears. For being so needy. So noticeably. For being unable to cope with one stupid little camping trip.

Actually, the kids had a great time. So did Wes. Face painting and puddle splashing and tractor rides with their very best friends. I got the sleep, and the rest, and the uninterrupted hours of solitude that I so desperately needed.

It still took me a week to realise that maybe, just maybe, I hadn't actually failed.

A few days after camp I got a message from a dear, dear friend. Letting me know how proud she was of me for leaving the field that night. For going home and being where

I needed to be. For throwing my hands up and admitting that I just couldn't cope.

She wrote about my decision with words like freedom. And wisdom. As though I hadn't just escaped, but consciously made a choice to go somewhere helpful.

At the time, in that tent, while my children refused to sleep and I shivered in a damp, sobbing pile of misery, I didn't think I had a choice. Wes wanted to take me home. So I went.

But I could have stayed. I could have stuck it out. That's usually my default. Fight. Don't give up. Don't let the side down.

Stay in the field.

It would have been disastrous. I would have gotten colder, and damper, and grumpier as the weekend wore on. I would have shouted at the children. Been short with my friends. Resentful of my husband. And for what?

To say I'd made it through. To martyr my way through yet another situation that I couldn't actually handle. To earn another worthless badge for my Supermummy sash.

Some things are worth fighting for. Marriages. Family. Mental health. Vocations. Community. Dignity.

Some things are not. I'm coming to the conclusion that there's only one way to fight for the big things. By not wasting your strength on the little ones.

I can't do everything. Nobody can. I need to stop pretending it's even a remote possibility.

I'm determined to embrace my real self. To get to know the woman that I actually am. I think I'm going to like her.

Next time church camp rolls around, I'll sign myself up as a day visitor. And I'll leave that field each evening with my head held high.

Almost as high as my umbrella.

Being your own cheerleader, or why mums are amazing.

I meet a lot of mums. It comes with the territory. There's not much choice when your major social outings consist of toddler groups, rhyme-times and the twice-daily trip to the nursery gate.

We talk. A lot. Despite our shared situation, we often don't have much in common. Our languages are different. As are our clothes. And our family set-ups. Even our approaches to the universal horror-story that is toddler bedtime. But one thing crops up. Over and over again. Guilt.

So many of our conversations revolve around it. We all feel guilty. Because we're working. Or because we're not. Because we're staying at home when we *only* have one child. Or two. Or four. Or eight.

I'm as guilty as the next mum. More, most days.

For instance. I decided this morning that today is a fish-fingers-and-chips-for-dinner sort of day. Since then I've spent hours trying not to guilt myself out of it. I've even had to write a meal plan for the week. To prove that I am going to cook 'properly' at least once. It's ludicrous.

I'm doing my best. We all are. It's just that, usually, we don't get much recognition. There's not a lot of cheerleading. I'll admit, I could be wrong on this one; it's hard to hear anything over the sound of Elvie singing the *Frozen* soundtrack on a continuous-high-pitched-thickly-American-accented-loop.

It got me thinking. Maybe we need to be our own cheerleaders. Sounds easy. It's not. Some days it's not even possible. But I think we need to try.

Mothers are amazing.

We make three different versions of dinner. To cater for

the child who doesn't eat spices, and the one who refuses anything that's ever set eyes on a potato. Despite the fact that we promised ourselves years ago that we would never be *that* mother.

We know the CBeebies schedule like the back of our hand. And are slowly introducing our offspring to the wonders of culture, sporting competition and culinary excellence. Thanks to *Strictly*, Wimbledon and *Masterchef*. It's purely for educational purposes. Of course.

We have an inbuilt protocol in the event of a code-brown-bath situation. Which mostly involves hoiking the children out of the water as soon as possible and leaving any contaminated bath toys in a bucket to be sterilised. Where they'll stay for about a week. Or however long it takes us to remember their existence.

We sit through tantrums. And more tantrums. And yet more tantrums. And we only occasionally take pictures. We have clothes (and faces) that are covered in glitter, paint, snot and old Weetabix. And we know that the fun the children are having makes it all worthwhile. Most of the time.

We know the difference between the pinky-purple bowl and the purply-pink bowl. And how critical that difference will be at snack time. We know how to play *Octonauts*, or 'little world' or duck, duck goose. Or whatever the pre-schooler is obsessed with this week. We only occasionally use sarcasm. When we're asked to play *Octonauts*. Again.

We wash all the dishes. And the clothes. And, occasionally, the bedding. Even though we know they'll just get dirty again. We can recite *The Gruffalo* in our sleep. Which comes in handy much more often than you'd think. We can translate the half-formed words of our toddlers. And conceal our disappointment when all they want to talk about is *Tree Fu Tom*. Or poo.

We lose our tempers. We say things we regret. And we apologise. And start again.

We have the words that calm nightmares.

The arms that rock babies to sleep.

The kisses that mend broken hearts.

Mothers are amazing.

Whether we have three children, or one, or seven. Whether we work outside the home or not. Regardless of whether we physically birthed our babies. Whatever our language. Or our faith. Or our opinion of the infamous 'naughty step'.

We are amazing.

Sometimes it's nice to be reminded.

Epilogue

Mysterious ways.

Today, I was a lady who lunches. Kind of.

Admittedly, it was sandwiches. At home. On paper plates. With four children under the age of four, and not enough chairs. The thought was there. And actually it was lovely.

We even managed a conversation. In between stopping the baby from climbing the stairs, and fending off a constant stream of demands; for biscuits, juice, or an afternoon off nursery.

We talked about depression. She knows a thing or two, this friend. She understands. We talked about medications. Family histories. About therapists and self-help books and well-meaning, helpfully-intentioned comments that fill you with an irrational and all-encompassing rage.

It was a good chat.

It's been weeks since I talked about my depression. Really, properly talked about it. How I'm coping. How it's going. How I feel. People don't want to pry and honestly, most of the time I'd rather discuss something else. Something a little cheerier. More light hearted. Something that's more likely to end with a joke.

The conversation took me by surprise. As did the revelation, halfway through, that my depression may yet be the making of me.

I said it off-hand. Almost a throwaway comment. It's only now, with hindsight, that I realise how true it is. And how totally unexpected.

Depression may yet be the making of me.

I don't say it lightly. Not this time. It's not coming from a Pinterest, cutesy-vintage-poster-with-an-uplifting-slogan kind of place. I'm not re-imagining the last few years through rose-tinted glasses. Not even slightly.

This is coming from a still-right-in-the-midst-of-it place. Where I'm swallowing down my tablets at breakfast and obsessively tidying at night in order to wake up to a clean slate in the morning. Where I turn down social invitations, often with half-truths or full-on inventions, because I can't face the effort of interacting. Where the panic over Wes going away starts a week before he leaves. And lasts until he returns. Where I could easily spend most of my day in bed. Most days.

Ignatian spirituality has a beautiful take on life's lowest moments. (Thank you book-group. Serious culture points.) It believes that depression, anxiety and even suicidal feelings, aren't wrong. Or bad. Or anything to be ashamed of. They see them as a signpost. A wake-up call. Nudging you towards a different way of life, when your current patterns have become totally unsustainable.

That's what's been happening to me. Much to my surprise.

Sometimes I wish that I wasn't so stubborn. That I could take a hint a little earlier. Spot the problems a little sooner. But that wouldn't have worked. I'd have carried on. Just as I was.

Trying to be perfect. Trying to make everyone around me perfect. Not accepting anything less. Perpetually disappointed. With myself and everything else. Crashing on from one month to the next, too frightened to stop for breath in case my life fell apart around me. Or I actually had to think.

I'm pretty sure that I would have ended up as a cranky,

uptight old lady. Without many friends. I certainly wouldn't have been friends with myself.

Depression is forcing me to change my future. It's taken me to the lowest point I could ever reach. And shown me that there's no way on earth I can ever be perfect. Or manage it all by myself. Not even close. That's been very hard to take. But thankfully there's another side to this rusty, battered old coin.

Little by little, depression is showing me grace. So much grace. From my friends. from my family, from my God. It's showing me that there are people who love me for who I am, not what I can do for them, or how beautifully my house is presented, or how many homemade desserts I serve at my lavish silver-plated dinner parties.

Thank goodness.

It's teaching me to lean on other people. Doctors. Family. Friends. Staff at the children's centre. Toddler group tea-ladies. Kindly middle-aged cashiers at supermarket checkouts.

It's teaching me to slow down. To take life one day at a time. That being four minutes late for nursery is absolutely worth it, if it avoids the vicious shoes-and-suncream fights that come when I rush everyone to be punctual.

It's teaching me that yoga and mindfulness are not just hippy crap. That actually, in the greater scheme of things, one-more-story-please is not the end of the world. That paint all over the floor/body/garden is a small price to pay for wild, unfettered creativity.

Above all, it's teaching me that I am ok. Just as I am. Quirks and all. That I should write, and paint, and play silly games. And all the other things I do well. That I should garden, and sew and build animals from Duplo. And all the other things I do very badly, but enjoy nonetheless.

It's showing me, ever so gently, that now I finally

understand a scrap of these truths for myself, I might actually stand a chance of passing them on to my children. Slowly but slowly but surely, depression is making me stronger. Making me able to face the world. As myself. Putting things into perspective, and nudging me in the direction of a calmer, happier, more positive life.

It's one hell of a tough teacher. I'm not going to argue with that. And it's nowhere near finished with me yet. But there's hope. So. Much. Hope.

God moves in mysterious ways. So the saying goes.

They don't get much more mysterious than this.

I hope.